Georgia's Colony of Roswell

One Man's Dream
And the People Who Lived It

Paulette Snoby

Paulette Snoby
RN, BSN, MPA

Interpreting Time's Past, LLC

Georgia's Colony of Roswell: One Man's Dream and the People Who Lived It.

Published by:
Interpreting Time's Past, LLC
Crab Orchard, Kentucky

Cover by Interpreting Time's Past, LLC

ISBN: 978-0-9964304-0-1

Contents

Acknowledgments

I owe a deep sense of gratitude to the people who provided clarification and pertinent historic truths that gives interest and substance to this manuscript. Many of these people are docents or educators of docents, who have told the Roswell story for many years. They lead tours, entertain the public, or portray a historic figure to educate school students. Most of us met at Fulton Teaching Museum North's program *Union Occupation of Roswell*. I am so grateful for their help but more importantly their friendship.

Stuart Arey, Roswell Historical Society (RHS) docent &
    King descendent
Amy Blalock, Smith Plantation docent and historian
Bill Browning, Special Events Coordinator,
    Barrington Hall
Jonathan Crooks, Rev. Pratt re-enactor & docent
Elaine DeNiro, Archivist of RHS Research Library
    and Archives
Michael Hitt, historian and author
Janet Johnson, RHS Cemetery Project Leader
Gwen Koehler, Education Coordinator, Bulloch Hall
Jena Sibille, Curator of Fulton Teaching Museum North
Robert Winebarger, Historic Site Coordinator,
    Barrington Hall

Several organizations house volumes of primary and secondary resources which were crucial to tracing the founding families' genealogy.

Georgia Historical Society, Savannah, Georgia
Georgia State Archives and History Department,
        Morrow, Georgia
Midway Museum and Archives, Midway, Georgia
Roswell Historical Society/City of Roswell Research
        Library and Archives

I am so thankful for all of the historical insight and research assistance from Connie Huddleston, a historical preservationist. Her publishing company, *Interpreting Times Past, LLC,* catered to my individual needs and wishes. Thank you Connie!

To my proofreader and editor, Ann Carstarphen, thank you for a job well done. See you on the golf course!

Dedication

I dedicate this book to all of my friends and family,
who encouraged me to write about
the most beautiful antebellum city in the South—
Roswell, Georgia.
Thank you!!!

Preface

Roswell, Georgia, has a rich history as a 19th century textile mill town. The six founding families brought their values, beliefs and customs from New England, Virginia, the Carolinas, and coastal Georgia to this frontier colony. Roswell's history reflects the growth and struggles of our young country after the War for Independence (Revolutionary War). It is a unique Southern town whose story is told over and over again to tourists, history lovers, children, and residents.

As docents for the Roswell Historical Society and Fulton Teaching Museum North, we relate the dreams and hopes of people from Roswell's beginnings. Our stories are filled with tales of conflict, intrigue, romance, daring, fortitude, and endurance. Many of the tales were passed down through generations, but are they true or conceived to add excitement and adventure to a myth from long ago?

Who were these pioneering families who came from the aristocratic Georgia coast? Who were their ancestors? Where did they come from? What caused their drive for adventure and exploration into an unknown Indian land? What happened to the previous landowners, the Cherokee Native Americans? Did the Union soldiers cause so much death and destruction that the Colony of Roswell would not survive? What about the millworkers earning just enough to feed and shelter their families? How did they survive the war?

These questions led me to research the people who built a Southern textile mill town hidden away in the Georgia foothills of the Appalachian Mountains. It was Roswell King's dream, but they lived it. Today, we are the beneficiaries of that dream living in a quiet Southern town raising our children and grandchildren.

Introduction

Many writers are driven by some quest when starting to do their research. Mine was to learn what happened in Connecticut that drove young Roswell King to leave his home. Those days during and after the Revolutionary War brought a sadness and despair that motived him to seek a happier life. I had other questions such as why he chose Darien, Georgia. Darien was just recovering from the British invasion and was not a prosperous town in 1789; perhaps Roswell King wanted to be the first among those who were rebuilding. We know that his life in Darien proved to be quite successful; he married, started a family, and explored various occupations and avenues to make a living.

I could not answer some other questions about Roswell's new life. For instance, how did Roswell and Catherine meet and what kind of courtship did they have? How did Roswell King meet Major Pierce Butler? Who convinced King to become the manager of Butler's large plantations on St. Simons Island? Why did Catherine remain in Darien and never visit her husband's colony, while Roswell lived and worked there for at least four years of her life before she died? What I did find is written under Part 1 The Entrepreneur.

Roswell King made very good business contacts with a majority of the coastal families he dealt with while living in Darien. This proved to be very helpful to him when the time came to seek out investors in the mill. They were the type of men who were willing to relocate their wives and children to the frontier, recently evacuated by the Cherokees. I saw the pioneering spirit grow within each generation as I traced each of these families' genealogies. I concluded that Roswell and Barrington chose men and women with adventurous spirits and a desire to make Roswell King's dream come true.

Parts 2 The Founding Families section contains family tree diagrams and descriptions of ancestors and descendants, which were painstakingly researched and documented. This research took me to the Midway Museum Archives in Midway, Georgia. Here I had the opportunity to examine letters written by King's great-grandchild, letters by his wife, Catherine, to Roswell King Jr., and letters from Catherine to Roswell about the progress of the mill. I also visited the graves and monuments of the Colonial Midway Cemetery, a touching and memorable experience.

At Savannah's Georgia Historical Society, I read about the Kings, Bullochs, Dunwodys, Elliotts, Stewarts, and Pratts, which added vital and accurate information to the families' backgrounds. I took the opportunity to visit Wormsloe Plantation, Fort Pulaski, and Fort McAllister. These places encouraged me to dig deeper into the lives of those who also knew these Georgia treasures.

Fortunately, the Georgia State Archives in Morrow contains the collection of Archibald Smith letters, journals, records etc. I spent hours reading what they wrote about how the Smiths' felt, how they lived, and what drove them from St. Mary's to Roswell.

I visited St. Simons Island several times and had conflicting feelings about the land development that essentially erased many of the antebellum plantations. Of course, the original houses were destroyed during the war, and by the effect that time has on all things made of tabby and lumber. I visited the ruins of the Butler Island rice fields and the housing development that obliterated Butler's Hampton Plantation. The Hamilton Plantation, now known as Epworth was preserved by the Methodist Center's dedication and occupancy.

Most distressing was the visit to Darien, once a busy port and a highly profitable trading center before the Union forces burned the city. Now Darien is a tiny modest village sitting along a lazy branch of the Altamaha River. Darien maintains its charm to entice tourists searching for the gateway to the Golden Isles.

The Roswell Historical Society's Archives and Library contains valuable primary and secondary resources, which form the foundation of this book. The King collection was insightful, but many documents were lost with the fire at Barrington Hall, where the collection was kept by descendants through the 20th century. Archivist, Elaine DeNiro, shared a wealth of knowledge about details that are now a part of some family's stories.

Bulloch Hall's archives provided clarification about the Bulloch family's early roots. Gwen Koehler, Education Coordinator, was very helpful in answering questions and providing research materials.

Part 3 Historical Buildings contains the description of the architecture, construction, and my photographs of the antebellum houses.

Part 4 The Textile Mills relates the history of the Roswell mills, the working conditions at the mills, and the damage that resulted from the invasion of the Union forces in 1864.

Part 5 Union Occupation is a summary of the three-week Union occupation of the Colony of Roswell. It is filled with pertinent details that make this event come alive for the reader. The fates of the millworkers are discussed in this section; it includes a timeline of their northern exile.

Each part has a section called *I Want To Know More About:*. These are detailed historical or geographical vignettes for the person who desires an in depth knowledge about certain topics found in that section.

I wrote this book to be an educational tool to train docents who lead tours of historic Roswell and the eighth grade Civil War program of the Fulton Teaching Museum North. I intended to write a resource with factual stories to intrigue tourists, students, and history lovers. I hope you are one of those!

Georgia's Colony of Roswell
One Man's Dream
And the People Who Lived It

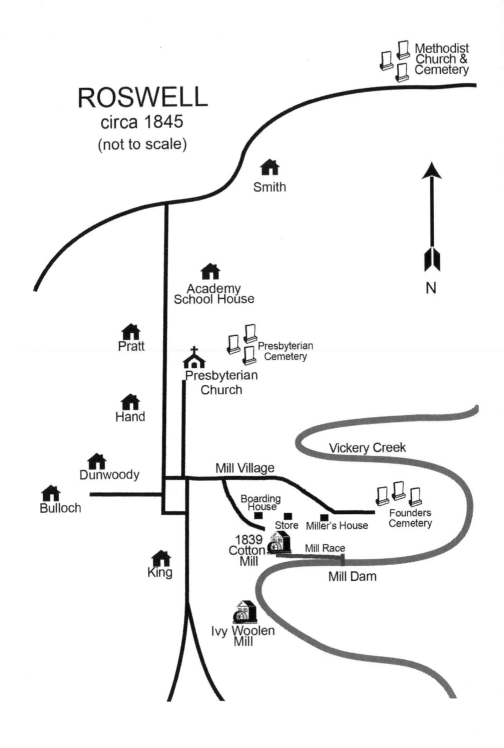

ROSWELL
circa 1845
(not to scale)

Methodist Church & Cemetery

N

Smith

Academy School House

Pratt

Presbyterian Cemetery

Presbyterian Church

Hand

Vickery Creek

Dunwoody

Mill Village

Bulloch

Boarding House

Founders Cemetery

Store   Miller's House

1839 Cotton Mill

Mill Race

King

Mill Dam

Ivy Woolen Mill

Part 1 The Entrepreneur

The Soldier

Roswell King, born on May 3, 1765, in Connecticut came from a large family of eleven siblings, typical for 18th century families. The Kings had a long remarkable history for patriotism; their ancestors trace back to Yorkshire, England, where they supported the English crown during the Irish rebellion.

Roswell's older brother joined the patriots early in the War for Independence. He was captured in 1777 and placed on a British prisoner of war ship. He died from a disease just as he gained his parole.

Roswell turned seventeen in 1782 and joined the patriotic cause as a private to fight the British. Fortunately, Roswell and his father, Timothy King, a captain of the American Brig *Defiance*, survived the war that ended in 1783.

As a fledgling new nation, the colonies fell under disastrous economic times. The depressed economy directly affected the King family's weaving business in Connecticut. Adding to their despair, Roswell's mother, Sarah, died in 1785. I suspect that these were two reasons for twenty-four-year-old Roswell to migrate south and begin a new life in Darien, Georgia, in 1789.

Moving South

Darien on the Altamaha River was beginning to rebuild itself into a thriving community after the evacuation of the British from its coastal waters in 1781. Roswell's move to Darien gave him opportunities to demonstrate his many skills and talents. He soon became a leader in the religious, civic, and business life extending from Savannah to St. Marys, Georgia.

Roswell had prior (minimal) military experience, and was elected to serve as lieutenant of the 2nd County Militia between 1793 and 1802. King successfully attempted many careers such as surveyor for Glynn County, Justice of the Peace, Justice of the Inferior Court of Glynn and McIntosh Counties, lumber measurer, and contractor to build Darien's twenty-room hotel. He held public office as a member of the Georgia House of Representatives in 1794-1795. King, a good money manager, became a landowner and broker of cotton and rice.

By 1792, King's reputation as an honorable and highly respected young man led to his marrying Catherine Barrington in Darien. Roswell and Catherine had ten children; three of those children died as infants or youths.

Catherine was the daughter of Lt. Colonel Josiah Barrington. Barrington was a friend and kinsman of General James Edward Oglethorpe, founder of the Colony of Georgia. Barrington's home was located on San Savilla Bluff, high above the Altamaha River, where Catherine was born. Fort Barrington was named for its commander, Lt. Col. Josiah Barrington. During the War for Independence, the fort was renamed Fort Howe when it was captured by the British.

Certainly, the most documented position Roswell held was manager and overseer of British Major Pierce Butler's estates on Butler's Point and St. Simons Island. Roswell's life seemed to be quite successful and his family was socially accepted among the Southern aristocracy. Tragedy struck this happy family after moving to Butler's estate, Hampton, when Roswell's infant son, Pierce Butler died. (His oldest son, Rufus, and their first daughter,

Catherine, died two years prior to the move. All three children were buried in Darien). Four more children were born while living on St. Simons Island including Thomas, William, Eliza, and Catherine Barrington.

While working on St. Simons Island, King managed several hundred slaves and oversaw the production of major crops of rice and cotton, which greatly increased Butler's wealth. King was an adaptable and very practical man in solving problems on the plantations. Catherine assisted with the responsibilities of running Hampton Plantation by managing the household slaves. King supervised the planting of crops and raising of cattle on Little St. Simons as well. Roswell King Jr. and Barrington worked with their father in later days on St. Simons Island.

King experimented with various plants and made good investment decisions for Butler; however, war with the British in 1812 changed King's life. During that war, the British emancipated one hundred and thirty-eight of Butler's slaves, which led to deterioration of the Butler-King relationship. King resigned in 1820 and became one of the Darien Bank directors.

An Adventure to Northern Georgia Mountains

In 1828, the Bank of Darien learned of the gold discovery near the town of Dahlonega. This was America's first gold rush. The bank's board of directors wanted to do business among the gold fields and decided to send Roswell King. He was chosen because of his reputation for strict integrity and fearlessness. King's mission was to open a bank and oversee its gold mining ventures located in north Georgia and North Carolina.

Roswell King, now sixty-five years old, agreed to travel in 1830 by horseback along North Carolina and Georgia Indian trails to arrive in Auraria near Dahlonega. Once the banking business was completed, King decided to return to Darien, sell his home

3

and businesses, and move to Auraria, Georgia. King decided to move because he wanted to buy gold for himself in 1831, as an investment opportunity.

While in the north Georgia mountains, King ventured out into the countryside to revisit (Cedar) Vickery Creek which he had noticed on his journey from the coast. The rushing waters of Vickery Creek reminded him of the New England streams, which provided the energy to power northern textile mills. Roswell began to form a vision of a southern textile mill, powered by water, as a profitable business venture where families invested, worked, and lived in a pleasant community.

This particular location had everything required to support a textile factory and a village. The climate was pleasant with no mosquitoes unlike coastal Georgia. The surrounding area was full of untapped resources of virgin pine, oak and hickory.

A few mill factories were already springing up in Georgia, and King saw a potential opportunity to make a lot of money. He decided right there and then he would make this dream happen; he wanted and needed his family and trusted business acquaintances to invest and move to north Georgia.

The next year, 1832, Georgia held a gold land lottery. King began to buy forty-acre lots from some lottery winners, who no longer wanted the land. Fannin Brown and Allen John Cole were individuals who sold their lottery lands in plot 266 to Roswell King. By 1838, King had acquired hundreds of acres to begin his dream.

Cherokee Nation

While Roswell King was building his dream among the pleasant foothills of the Appalachian Mountains, another people were struggling to survive the plans of the Federal and Georgia governments. These people were the Cherokees, who for hundreds of years had lived and died on this tribal land. The Cherokee Nation stretched between the Chattahoochee and Tennessee Rivers in one direction, and between the beginning of the Coosa and Tallapoosa Rivers in Alabama and the Hiawassee River in Tennessee. Living in the mountains, the Cherokees were out of the main path of white migration to the west. This allowed them to avoid removal from their land longer than the other major tribe in Georgia, the Creeks.

Unfortunately, more Georgians illegally entered Cherokee land with the gold discovery in 1828. This event proved to be the most influential factor that resulted in the confiscation and distribution of Cherokee land. The United States Army and several state militias removed the majority of Cherokees from their ancestral land in 1838. It became known as the *Trail of Tears* because of the deprivations and hardships the Cherokee people endured. More than four thousand of the fifteen thousand Cherokees died during this forced march to the new Indian territories, located in the Oklahoma Territory and Arkansas.

Georgia instituted a land lottery system to distribute land taken from the Cherokee Nation. Many of those who won the lottery lost interest when the gold mines no longer produced and sold their plots. The Colony of Roswell sits on such land. Fifteen Cherokee families who lived along Vickery Creek were sent on the *Trail of Tears*. Some of the gold diggings were abandoned for agriculture or sold to others as early as December 1838.

Beginning of A Dream

Roswell King returned to Darien and convinced his son, Barrington, to share his dream. Barrington became intrigued as over the last few years, his income from cotton was decreasing. This was because the soil had become depleted of nutrients from

5

growing cotton for many years; therefore, the land yielded less and less profit.

Barrington realized that the idea of the Colony of Roswell offered a new way of life for his family. This new lifestyle could provide a healthier environment in a self-contained village setting. Barrington's children could be raised in the Presbyterian manner he desired for them. He agreed to travel with his father to inspect the land along Vickery Creek. Seeing the land and all it had to offer encouraged King's son to make his father's dream his own.

The decision was made and Roswell soon began building the Colony's infrastructure. He hired local workmen and arranged for slaves to build roads, a dam, and a sawmill. Next, Roswell had a log cabin built for his son's family, who will join him in the Colony. Ralph King, another son, helped to build the cotton mill (factory), which became operational in 1838.

Meanwhile, Barrington quickly returned to the Georgia coast to inspire a selected group of men to invest in the mill and bring their families to live in the Colony. He explained that Roswell was clearing the land, laying out roads, and building a sawmill and dam to provide for a water-powered textile mill on Vickery Creek. He told them his father was recruiting yeoman farmers from Virginia, North and South Carolina, and Georgia to the Colony of Roswell. They will grow cotton to process at the King's mill. The raw cotton grown near the mill will be manufactured into cotton thread, woven into yarn and cloth, and sold as a finished product in Southern cities, New England, France, and England. This concept eliminated the middleman, so profits for the mill owners were predicted to increase dramatically.

Barrington enticed the selected few families by providing sixteen acres of land, a home site, and an option to buy stock in the mill company. Many of them viewed King's dream as a refuge from the sick seasonal months, when malaria and mosquitoes plagued coastal Georgia. The Colony would be a permanent haven to educate and raise their families in a secluded safe environment.

By 1839, the Colony's founding families included Roswell and Barrington King, Elizabeth King Hand, John Dunwody, James S. Bulloch, Reverend Nathaniel A. Pratt, and Archibald Smith. The families left Savannah, Midway, Darien, Sunbury, and St. Marys to accept King's offer. Many eventually will sell their coastal holdings.

Roswell homes were built around the "park" or village square that resembled a New England town common. Roswell King envisioned wide and clean streets with beautiful Greek Revival homes on the west side of the square. The mill factory, shops, and workers' homes were located on the east side of the square.

Roswell further designated and donated land for the building of the Presbyterian Church, and a schoolhouse. (Years later Barrington King donated land for a Methodist Church). Roswell King also planned homes for the millworkers. He built a two-building complex of apartments, *The Bricks,* and individual and duplex clapboard dwellings for the millworkers.

As a practical man, Roswell had a company store built near the mill site; he traveled to New York City to make special financial arrangements to purchase goods to stock that store. The store opened two weeks after the mill became operational in 1839. Eventually in 1842, King hired a young man from Utica, New York to run the company store; he eventually became an agent for the mill company. This same man, George Hull Camp, became president of the Roswell Manufacturing Company after Barrington King's death. Camp later was one of the many owners of Primrose Cottage, previously Elizabeth Hand's home built by Roswell King.

Roswell Manufacturing Company store, author's photograph

The Georgia Assembly incorporated the Roswell Manufacturing Company (RMC) on December 11, 1839, with Barrington as its first president. The RMC built other spinning factories and gristmills over the next ten years. Eventually a gristmill, located in Lebanon (north of Roswell), a woolen mill, a flour mill, and the Willeo mill ran under RMC's charter. By 1860, there were four to five hundred millworkers employed by Roswell King's RMC.

On To Roswell

The families who agreed to come to northwest Georgia traveled in coaches and wagons loaded with furniture and supplies along an ancient trail known as Hightower Indian Trail.

They crossed the Chattahoochee River by ferry and then up the bluff to reach the land King was developing. The journey from the coast took at least two weeks.

Lebanon was a small trading center two miles north of the Colony. It had already been established in 1832. Lebanon consisted of a store, gristmill, and post office. Further north, another community existed called New Prospect Camp Ground or Methodist Campground. Now called Alpharetta, it became one of the fastest growing towns in the South.

The six founding families started to arrive in the spring of 1838. The newcomers experienced many hardships as they settled among the virgin forests. For most, this was their first move from the homes their colonial ancestors settled a century or more ago. Each husband and wife had to manage ordinary cases of fever and minor surgery. The Kings made no provision for a resident physician; the nearest qualified doctor was fourteen miles away.

The land was beautiful; it also supplied what the families needed to survive. The forest provided an abundance of game and the sparkling streams were filled with fish and turtles to add to their diet. While the families lived in modest temporary dwellings, they continued to practice the ways of their refined culture. They dressed for suitable occasions such as Sunday service, evening dinner, and party gatherings.

New homes were started once the Presbyterian Church and school house were built. Roswell King sought a pastor who would prepare the young men for college. One such gifted minister was the Reverend Nathaniel A. Pratt, husband of Catherine King Pratt, Roswell's daughter. Religion was extremely important to the families and an integral part of their daily lives. They read the Presbyterian catechism, sang the standard hymns, and memorized scripture. Family prayers were said both morning and evening and included their enslaved African families.

The first family to arrive in the spring of 1838 was Barrington and Catherine King; they chose land on the highest hill overlooking the mills at the square's south end. Soon to follow, Major James and Martha Bulloch chose a ten-acre site west of the square with a view of a beautiful, plush valley, and a mountain in the distance (Kennesaw). John and Jane Dunwody followed the Bullochs and chose a site adjacent to James and Martha. Their children played together on the village square. Jane Dunwody and James Bulloch were siblings, and many of the children were first cousins.

During the autumn of 1838, Roswell's daughter, Elizabeth King Hand, informed him of her husband's sudden demise. She was determined to come to the Colony no matter. Her father instructed the builders to quickly complete Elizabeth's home; it was begun in January 1839. This was the first permanent home built in Roswell and was completed by August 1839. Roswell King moved into Primrose Cottage with Elizabeth and her children, and he remained there until his death in February 1844.

The Smiths arrived in the Colony during December 1839, from St. Marys not long after Elizabeth Hand. The Smiths came for the promise of rich farmland and to invest in the mill company. Their temporary home was located in the Lebanon area on land they bought called Oakwood Farm; it continued to be farmed by Smith's many slaves even after the new home was completed.

The last arrivals were Reverend Nathaniel and Catherine Pratt in early 1840. Once the Darien Church released Pratt as minister, he accepted the new position to shepherd the Roswell's Presbyterian flock. His home was located diagonally from the Presbyterian Church, beside the school house called the Academy built in 1840. Reverend A. H. Hand taught at the Academy until 1870, when the school was given to the city because of the increased number of students.

Roswell King was successful in locating farmers to supply cotton for the mill. He and Barrington also recruited families to work in the mill factory. These people were housed in rentals built along Factory Hill, which covered forty acres of the village. Factory Hill is located east of the village square along today's Sloan Street. The mill workers were white, working folk who paid rent to live in a Roswell Manufacturing Company house. Their allotted home size was based on the number of children and adults who worked at the mill. Slaves were considered too valuable to be millworkers, since the equipment could cause serious physical injury. A few skilled slaves occasionally fixed any broken mill machinery or acted as mill security guards.

The founding families and millworkers were not the only white settlers in the area, as families already resided in the surrounding hills and valleys. These upland farmers were quite different from the low country planters. Most were poor, white, illiterate, but hospitable. They spent their lives hunting, trapping, fishing, and farming on very poor soil. Few were slave owners; some found their way to Roswell to work in the mills.

Building Mansions

Barrington King hired Willis Ball, a Connecticut master builder, to design and supervise the building of several homes including Barrington Hall, Bulloch Hall, Dunwody Hall, and the Presbyterian Church. Most of the coastal families chose the popular Greek Revival style architecture inspired by ancient Greek temples. Thomas Jefferson introduced this style when he returned from France. This architecture was used for the executive mansion (later called the White House) and the University of Virginia in Charlottesville.

The building began once the homes were designed, lumber seasoned, and craftsmen located. Skilled slaves with talents for carpentry and masonry were sought, while other craftsmen were hired to do the intricate woodworking that graces those mansions today. Many pieces of furniture were handcrafted by skilled slaves and handed down through generations. Bricks for homes and the mill were handmade by slaves from clay harvested from the banks of creeks and the Chattahoochee River. Barrington King owned the kilns where the bricks were fired. The timber for framing was cut from nearby forests. It had to be aged between one and two years before used in framing the homes. Heart of pine was sought for flooring and highly valued to prevent insect infestation.

Other families will later build homes in the Colony but were not the first founders and investors in Roswell King's dream, which was now becoming a reality. Unfortunately, Roswell's wife, Catherine Barrington, never saw the result of her husband's labors. She died in 1839 in Darien far from Roswell.

Roswell Square (Founders Square)

The village square or park was built for Roswell residents to gather socially, conduct political meetings, have picnics, and provide a safe place for children to play. The original Roswell Manufacturing Company Store was a two-story building built in 1839 close to the mill. Each time the store was expanded, it moved farther away from the mill up toward the square. Finally its 1854 location faced the east side of the square. In the 20th century, the store expanded to house a post office, a telephone exchange, and annex. The annex contained a funeral home, soda shop, and the first movie theater in Roswell.

The company store sold fine hats, linen coats, pistols, gunpowder, tobacco, and tools to the gentlemen. Ladies bought French calico, gloves, bonnets, ribbons, Swiss muslins, combs, and brushes. Millworkers used RMC printed-paper money or script to pay for housewares, ointments, oil lamps, coffee, and flatware. When the company store closed, the building held various restaurant chains throughout the 20th century.

The village square contains a 1905 period bandstand replica, built to commemorate the visit of President Theodore Roosevelt Jr. In the 1930's, the Works Progress Administration (WPA) installed a fountain in the center of the square; it would later be replaced in 1976 by a newer version. On June 1, 2010, the City of Roswell replaced the 1976 fountain with an obelisk made of Elberton granite to honor the town's founder, Roswell King. This obelisk and fountain were created to resemble King's gravestone monument, which still exists in the Founders Cemetery.

Gazebo on the Square, author's photograph

King's Obelisk on the Square,
author's photograph

Sloan Street or Factory Hill Street

The Bricks

Roswell Manufacturing Company built two apartment complexes, *The Bricks*. Each complex contained ten apartments and are thought to be the Southeast's oldest apartments. *The Bricks* overlook Vickery Creek and the mill village along Sloan Street once called Factory Hill Street. Each apartment has a combined kitchen and dining room on the lower floor and one bedroom upstairs. Today, they are privately-owned condominiums, which were expanded and restored with modern conveniences. *The Bricks* have been in continual use since 1840.

The Bricks, author's photograph

Millworker Homes

The Roswell Manufacturing Company built single or duplex homes for mill workers to rent while they were employees. Today, many of those houses have disappeared, but a few remain along Sloan Street as privately restored residences or small businesses. During the early 1800's, many of these families wandered from mill to mill; when work slowed in one mill, they traveled to another as work became available. This would disqualify them from renting a house from RMC, unless they were employed at one of its mills.

Millworker's duplex, author's photograph

Cemeteries
Founders Cemetery

Where there is life, death will eventually follow. Death does not play favorites; it takes both the rich and poor, young and old. In the case of the Colony of Roswell families, death came in 1841 with a scarlet fever epidemic. Four children from three founding families contracted the disease; they did not survive. The death of Charles Irvine Bulloch, age 2 years and 9 months, caused the town to designate a public burial site in 1841. Once called Presbyterian Cemetery, then Old Presbyterian Cemetery, it is known today as the Founders Cemetery. It is thought the first boundaries were north of Sloan Street, east of Walnut Street, and bound by Vickery Creek in the south.

The next children to succumb to the fever during July of 1841 were Barrington King's children, Nephew (11 years old) and Susan (9 years old). These children died and were buried on Founders Cemetery knoll. Ralph King Hand, son of Elizabeth King

16

Hand, who had recently arrived in Roswell, was the last founder's child to die in November 1841, at age 3. Children of millworkers also died from the fever, but their names are not recorded for us to know.

Many significant people were buried in this cemetery including Major James Stephens Bulloch, John Dunwody, Jane Dunwody, Georgia Amanda Elliott (Martha Bulloch's daughter), and Horace Southworth Pratt (brother of Reverend Nathaniel A. Pratt).

Roswell King joined his three grandchildren in Founders Cemetery on February 14, 1844, but his dream lived on in the people who had made Roswell their home.

Roswell King grave monument,
author's photograph

Once Roswell Presbyterian Church Cemetery was created, the gentry no longer used Founders Cemetery for burials. The millworkers and slaves continued to find a place of rest in unmarked graves within the Founders Cemetery. The last recorded burial there was James A. Burney, son of Dr. P.J. Burney, born October 13, 1850, and died on May 18, 1860.

During the Civil War, residents claimed Union soldiers disturbed Roswell King's grave site searching for valuables. Vandalism may be one of the reasons that Founders Cemetery's location lost its appeal for future burials. James R. King, Roswell's grandson and Barrington's son, ordered the removal of the founding family's four children's graves from Founders Cemetery. These graves are now located in the Roswell Presbyterian Church Cemetery.

Roswell Presbyterian Church Cemetery

This cemetery was established in 1841 by the church and was located about three hundred feet behind the sanctuary. Atlanta Street cuts through the land thus separating the cemetery from the church property. Today, the cemetery is located at the intersection of Atlanta Street and Oak Street. It has about two hundred graves and a memorial garden; the cemetery still accepts burials.

Many notables are buried here including Confederate soldiers and founding family members. Some of them are Major Charles A. Dunwody; Major Henry Dunwody and his wife and three children; Barrington King and his wife Catherine; Col. Barrington Simeral King; Captain Thomas E. King, James R. King and Francis, his wife; Archibald Smith, Anne Magill, his wife, both daughters Eliza and Helen; Reverend Nathaniel A. Pratt and his wife Catherine; and Daniel S. Elliott (Martha Bulloch's son). The four children from Founders Cemetery also rest here. Frances

Fanny Whitmire and her mother, both millworkers, are buried here. They were members of the church and played a significant role in hiding the church's silver from the Union troops in 1864.

Old Roswell Cemetery (or Methodist Church Cemetery)

This cemetery was established in 1846 and associated with the Mount Carmel Methodist Church, which no longer exists. The log-cabin church ministered to its congregation from 1836 to 1845. It was located at the intersection of Woodstock Road and Alpharetta Highway. The oldest legible gravestone is of a four-month-old child who was buried in 1846. The plots are privately owned, and the cemetery remains available for burials.

Veterans from the Civil War, World War I, World War II, Korean, and Vietnam Wars are interred here. There are eighteen known Confederate soldiers in the cemetery.

The Roswell Historical Society's Cemetery Committee is cleaning, repairing, and digitally documenting the graves and monuments. United States military veterans buried in the cemeteries are remembered by various local patriotic and genealogical organizations. American flags are placed on the graves and ceremonies are held on Memorial Day and Independence Day. Confederate soldiers are remembered in April with Confederate National flags placed by the Sons of Confederate Veterans, Roswell Mills Camp.

The 1839 Mill

King's first cotton mill (referred to as the 1839 mill) operated with three thousand, five hundred spindles and forty looms. The mill complex consisted of a three-story brick building (factory), machine shop, office, and a company store. This mill worked efficiently and finally reached its capacity. RMC decided to expand, and an addition was built which increased the mill's output. This first mill became part of a well-run complex until it was completely burned by Union troops in July 1864; it would not be rebuilt.

I WANT TO KNOW MORE ABOUT:

POST-REVOLUTIONARY WAR ECONOMY

The thirteen colonies in 1783 united as a new nation. The new country faced terrible economic situations immediately after the war. This economic crisis came as a result of restriction of exports to Britain and their Caribbean sugar colonies. As a result, the two major sources of commerce for the states were eliminated.

At the same time, there was a flood of cheaply made goods imported from Britain. American-made goods could not compete and caused personal hardship for American-owned businesses.

Connecticut strongly felt the impact of the American economy's instability and its failing currency. Revolutionary War soldiers and sailors could not pay their bills and their mortgages, as the American dollar decreased in value. Anarchy and armed conflict resulted with foreclosure of farms and frontier property. The flood of cheap British goods harmed Connecticut factories, and many textile owners and weavers lost their businesses.

Each of the colonies assumed a high level of debt from the funding of the recent war. All of these circumstances increased the rapid inflation inflicted upon the new country and its people. The future of the fledging republic was threatened.

DARIEN, GEORGIA

Darien is located thirty miles south of Midway, Georgia, on the Darien River, the northern branch of the Altamaha River. The Ocmulgee and the Oconee Rivers feed the Altamaha River; these rivers drain water from upper and middle Georgia. The Altamaha meanders through marshes before its waters find the Atlantic Ocean between St. Simons and Sapelo Islands.

Darien was once a bustling port and a leading lumber town in Georgia. It was the site of a large Creek Village before white settlers arrived. By 1721, the British built Fort King George on Darien's bluff to protect England's colony of Carolina. The first white settlers of Georgia were Scottish Highlanders who arrived with Hugh MacKay in 1736. General James Oglethorpe brought them to defend Georgia and the Carolinas from the Spanish located in Florida. Initially, the village was called New Inverness, the name Darien was later chosen in memory of other Presbyterian Scots, who failed to establish a 1699 Scottish settlement in Panama.

General James Edward Oglethorpe, the military leader of Darien, led an expedition in 1739 against the Spanish in St Augustine. This proved disastrous for many highlanders who lost their lives. Fort Barrington was constructed in 1751, near Darien, as protection from the Native Americans and later the British. No trace remains of the fort today.

Pre-Civil War Darien had a hospital, churches, a public school, several private schools, and academies. It boasted of two hotels and a bank, the leading financial institution for the state of Georgia. Thomas Spalding was elected as bank president; he stated that the bank was the strongest financial institution south of Philadelphia, Pennsylvania. It was half-owned and partially controlled by the state government, with a branch in Milledgeville and six others throughout Georgia. (Milledgeville was capital of Georgia during this time). There was much political controversy surrounding the bank, which existed for only twenty-two years.

Darien was a thriving town in 1863 with eighty homes, twelve stores, five churches, some mills with storehouses, a courthouse, dispensary, saloons, bookstore, schoolhouse, and a jail. There were five hundred whites and fifteen hundred Negroes residing within Darien and the immediate surrounding area. The bustling little town met its temporary demise when Federal troops, including United States Colored Troops, set fire to the town in June 1863. The people fled to the Ridge, which was nearby, and remained living there for the next five years. Darien was in a state of ruin with only three houses surviving. The Methodist church was set ablaze but refused to burn. Later the church was destroyed in 1881 by a hurricane and replaced in 1883 with the present sanctuary. The church served as one of the rallying points for Darien's rebuilding.

One Darien resident, Reuben King, remained in his home when Union troops arrived in the area. Reuben had followed his brother, Roswell King, to Darien from Connecticut. Reuben was a tanner and had bought Mallow Plantation on the Sapelo River at Pine Harbor Bluff early in the 19th century. He and his wife were living on the plantation when Federal gunboats raided the town in 1862. Mallow Plantation originally was a royal grant given to Captain John McIntosh, a British Army officer who served in Florida during the War with Spain. After the Revolutionary War, Captain William McIntosh owned Mallow; he was the father of the Indian Chief, General William McIntosh by his Creek wife Senoya.

Today, Darien is a very small coastal village whose existence depends on tourism and surrounding farming trade.

THE SOUTH'S ECONOMY DURING THE 1840S

An economic depression in 1840 spread throughout the agricultural south. It started around coastal Georgia and included the delta near Darien. Cotton prices dropped dramatically, and rice profits were at the mercy of the weather. Crops were ruined by hurricane or drought. Southern prosperity returned by the 1850's, as industrialization with mills and diversifications were adopted.

CHEROKEE NATIVE AMERICANS

Late in the 18th century, George Washington introduced a program to "civilize" the Native Americans. They would gradually assimilate into American society. This assimilation included private land ownership (no longer tribal ownership) and patriarchal households. The Cherokees and other tribes were to replace hunting for farming and raising of cattle. Any land not in use was distributed to white European settlers.

As the 18th century progressed, Georgia settlers encroached upon Native American lands through various secret agreements, bribery, and negotiations after the ending of the Indian wars. The Cherokees resided in eighty towns stretching along rivers and streams. They owned farms, plantation-style homes, mills, and shops. The Cherokee Nation had its own government, constitution, alphabet, and newspaper. The centralized government was located at the Cherokee national capital of New Echota in Georgia. These people realized their only chance for survival, with the encroachment of the European whites, was to emulate them in their ways and culture. The Cherokee became the most civilized and progressive tribe in the United States at that time.

Early in her history, Georgia claimed land from the coast across Alabama and Mississippi to the Mississippi River. Congress, in 1798, decided the area between the Chattahoochee and Mississippi Rivers would be called the Mississippi Territory. It would have its own government and no longer be a part of Georgia. Four years later, Georgia agreed and transferred that land to the Federal Government for $1,250,000 and a promise by the Federals to remove all remaining Native Americans from Georgia.

More Cherokees adopted ways of the Southern white populace and owned African slaves. By 1819, there were fifteen thousand Cherokees and two hundred enslaved African Americans at the time the American Congress passed the Indian Removal Act of 1830.

A small group of Cherokees consisting of John Ridge, his son, Elias Boudinot, and Stand Watie approached the Federal Government to willingly sell Cherokee land and peaceably move to the designated Indian Territory for five million dollars. Agreeing to this arrangement, the Treaty of New Echota was signed by these four men. According to Cherokee law, they had no right to sell the land, and they were not members of the tribal council. Eventually, three of the four men were brutally murdered by their own people once settled in Oklahoma Territory; Stand Watie was warned and survived the assassination attempt.

Other Cherokees fought against the Indian Removal act politically by bringing a lawsuit to the United States Supreme Court, which ruled in their favor. However, President Andrew

Jackson denounced the court ruling and gave his approval to forcibly remove all Cherokees from their homeland. By 1832, Georgia had successfully defied the Supreme Court with the Georgia Guard enforcing the new Indian Removal Act. A land lottery was held, and the white Georgians permanently settled into Northwest Georgia.

By May of 1838, the Federal Government and Georgia militia had built sixteen forts in Georgia to receive the remaining Cherokees prior to embarkation points in Tennessee. General Winfield Scott was charged with gathering fifteen thousand Cherokees using the United States Army. In Georgia, the forts were located in present day counties of Bartow, Polk, Floyd, Gordon, Murray, Gilmer, Walker, Towns, Lumpkin, Forsyth, Cherokee, and Pickens. There were four additional forts in congruent states. (Fort Marr is the only remaining fort today and is located in Benton, Tennessee). The conditions at the forts were horrible. The Cherokees were physically abused, deprived of adequate shelter, and starved. The round up of the Cherokees ended on June 2, 1838, but the ordeal was just beginning for the people.

Two embarkation points were Rattlesnake Springs, near Cherokee Agency, Tennessee, and Ross's Landing, Chattanooga, Tennessee. The water route beginning at Ross's Landing was by steamship west along the Tennessee River down the Mississippi River to the Arkansas River to Fort Smith and then northwest by land to Arkansas.

The land route was technically known as "The Trail of Tears" from Rattlesnake Springs to Nashville, Tennessee, and then Hopkinsville, Kentucky. The Cherokee crossed the Ohio River and moved southwest to cross the Mississippi

River. They walked southwest to the Ozark Plateau to the Oklahoma Territory.

The army and state militia groups marched the Cherokees twelve hundred miles to their new homeland. Four thousand Cherokees died of disease as a result of the hardship during the journey. A few Cherokee escaped to the mountains of Western North Carolina. Their descendants reside today on the Qualla Reservation outside of Cherokee, North Carolina.

The Georgia Legislature granted full citizenship to twenty-two Cherokee families of mixed blood living on old Cherokee lands. These families had to buy back their land from the lottery winners.

Part 2 Founding Family Roots

Who were these people and what made them so remarkable in Roswell's history? I searched each family's genealogical tree and discovered that their roots were deeply embedded in England, Scotland, or Ireland.

There were several common factors among the families. Each family contained at least one ancestor who willingly migrated to the British colonies. Those who took the risk became active participants in their new community; they raised families and joined military units to defend their new homes. Patriotism was a value handed down through the generations, and it was strongly demonstrated by descendants who fought in the War for Independence (American Revolutionary War) and later the War of the Rebellion (American Civil War).

Another element that came to my attention was that their early ancestors were willing to leave New England, and the Middle and Southern Colonies. They resettled in the Province of Georgia, knowing that attacks by the Spanish or Indians were possible. Later their descendants were willing to leave behind the safety of their coastal estates and venture into an unknown land. Their motives were to increase the family wealth and to provide a healthier lifestyle for their children.

Primary documents revealed these families intermingled through marriage, and frequently, family surnames were chosen as first or middle names of their children. An example of this is Roswell and Catherine Barrington King naming their son,

Barrington. These people were proud of their heritage. Families also used the same names over and over again, which makes it so very difficult to understand who is who. Therefore, the genealogical diagrams are placed among the pages of the family written about, for the reader's convenience.

One additional common trait was including family members, such as first, second, or third cousins, in business enterprises. They continued to build strong and lasting friendships among themselves. Many of these family/business relationships resulted in marriages. These coastal families professed the Presbyterian faith; although some were members of the Midway Congregational Church, others joined the Independent Presbyterian Church of Savannah, or the Presbyterian Church in Darien, Georgia.

A. Roswell King's Yorkshire Roots

The King family was known by the other Colony founders as *The Royal Family*. They thought this name was a play on the word, King; however, they were not so far from the truth. The ancient seat or castle of the Kings was Feathercock Hall of Yorkshire, England.

Roswell King's ancestor, Lord Edward King of County York was the first Archbishop of York during the Protestant Reformation. Lord Edward's family acquired many rich estates and gained recognition from the royals because of their military service during the Nine Years' War with Ireland. Lord Edward's relative, Sir John King, served in the Nine Years' War and received knighthood from Queen Elizabeth. After her death, King James I further awarded Sir John King with Irish land in 1603 at Roscommon, Roscommon County, Ireland. As part of the grant, he received the 12th century Abbey of Boyle. Sir John was given

28

these estates because he forced the Irish to obey anti-Catholic penal laws through violent subjugation and enforcement. He married Catherine Drury, daughter of Robert Drury, who also helped to suppress the Irish rebellion. It is apparent that the King family's English line was loyal to the crown at the expense of the Irish.

Sir John and Catherine's second son (Sir) John King II was knighted and appointed Secretary of Ireland for England. He married Margaret Edgeworth and sired five sons. Robert King was the oldest son and heir to the Irish barony title of Kingston. His sons became the Irish branch known as Earls of Kingston.

Sir John and Catherine's second son, John, born in Ireland in 1629, was left with no title or inheritance, which was the custom of the day. Please note that John was an Englishman, born to English parents. John attended school in Northampton, England. Once his father died in 1644, John had little choice but to migrate to the British Colonies in 1645, at sixteen years of age.

Upon arrival in the Province of Massachusetts, John quickly found his place in the community as one of the founders of Northampton and Northfield, Massachusetts. He joined the militia and defended the colony against hostile Native Americans, and acquired a captaincy in the process. John did well and married Sarah Holton in 1656, whose father was also one of the founders of Northampton. They had ten children; Captain John King's family included one grandson Thomas King Jr., the grandfather of Roswell King.

(Captain) Timothy King (1727-1812) married Sarah Fitch in 1736 and sired eleven children. They were the parents of Roswell King, our town's founder. Captain King became a naval hero during the American Revolutionary War, as he commanded the Brig *Defiance*. Roswell's uncle, John Fitch, was quite an inventor and entrepreneur; he developed a steam engine, which he used in his business. Roswell seemed to have inherited John's visionary trait.

King Yorkshire Roots

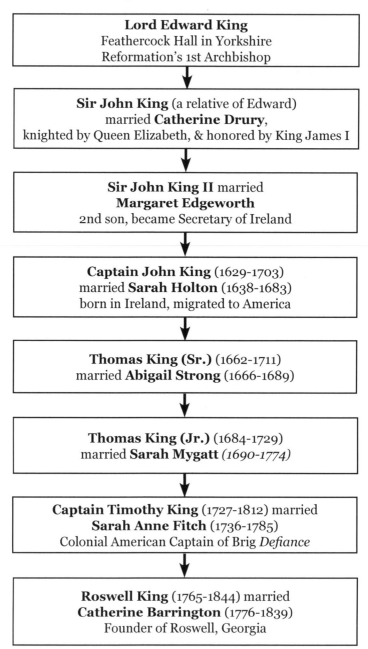

Lord Edward King
Feathercock Hall in Yorkshire
Reformation's 1st Archbishop

↓

Sir John King (a relative of Edward)
married **Catherine Drury**,
knighted by Queen Elizabeth, & honored by King James I

↓

Sir John King II married
Margaret Edgeworth
2nd son, became Secretary of Ireland

↓

Captain John King (1629-1703)
married **Sarah Holton** (1638-1683)
born in Ireland, migrated to America

↓

Thomas King (Sr.) (1662-1711)
married **Abigail Strong** (1666-1689)

↓

Thomas King (Jr.) (1684-1729)
married **Sarah Mygatt** *(1690-1774)*

↓

Captain Timothy King (1727-1812) married
Sarah Anne Fitch (1736-1785)
Colonial American Captain of Brig *Defiance*

↓

Roswell King (1765-1844) married
Catherine Barrington (1776-1839)
Founder of Roswell, Georgia

Fitch Roots

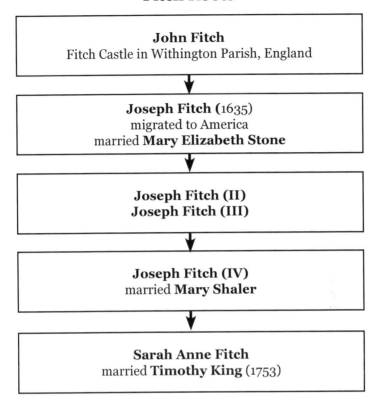

John Fitch
Fitch Castle in Withington Parish, England

↓

Joseph Fitch (1635)
migrated to America
married **Mary Elizabeth Stone**

↓

Joseph Fitch (II)
Joseph Fitch (III)

↓

Joseph Fitch (IV)
married **Mary Shaler**

↓

Sarah Anne Fitch
married **Timothy King** (1753)

B. Roswell and Catherine King

Roswell King (1765-1844) married Catherine Barrington (1776-1839) on April 14, 1792, at her father's San Savilla Bluff Plantation. Her parents, Josiah and Sarah Williams Barrington, lived fifteen miles from Darien on the Altamaha River. Roswell and Catherine had ten children; six were born on St. Simons Island, one in Savannah, and three in Darien. Sadly, three of their children died as youths.

Catherine never saw Roswell's dream fulfilled; she died in 1839 in Darien and was buried at the Ridge beside her sister, Eliza. Later Catherine's grave was moved to St. Andrews Cemetery in Darien. The Ridge is a historic site located in Ridgeview, Georgia, north of Darien.

Barrington Roots

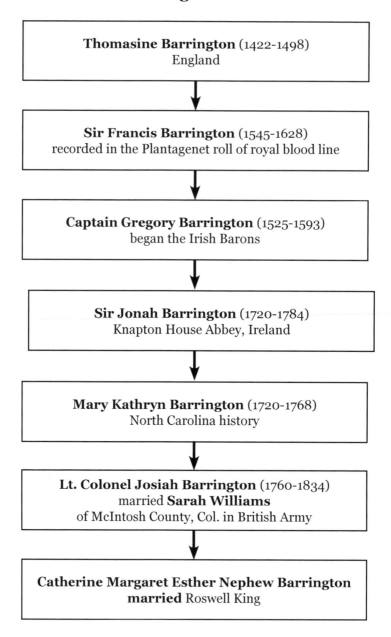

Thomasine Barrington (1422-1498)
England

Sir Francis Barrington (1545-1628)
recorded in the Plantagenet roll of royal blood line

Captain Gregory Barrington (1525-1593)
began the Irish Barons

Sir Jonah Barrington (1720-1784)
Knapton House Abbey, Ireland

Mary Kathryn Barrington (1720-1768)
North Carolina history

Lt. Colonel Josiah Barrington (1760-1834)
married Sarah Williams
of McIntosh County, Col. in British Army

Catherine Margaret Esther Nephew Barrington
married Roswell King

Roswell and Catherine raised interesting children and the following is a short summary of each child's life.

Roswell King Jr.

Roswell King Jr. was the second son born to the Kings (1796-1854); he was not an investor or resident of Roswell. He married Julia Rebecca Maxwell, daughter of Audley Maxwell, who ran a highly prosperous plantation in Liberty County, named Carnichfergus. Roswell King Jr. purchased South Hampton Plantation, Woodville, and Yellow Bluff on Colonel's Island near Savannah for his family.

We know his history as manager of the Butler estates on St. Simons Island, which Frances Anne Kemble wrote about in *Journal of a Residence on a Georgian Plantation* in 1838-1839. He assisted his father with management of these estates until his father resigned; he later agreed to become manager of those estates. He efficiently oversaw seven hundred people (slaves) and large tracts of land. In 1838, Roswell King Jr. left St. Simons Island to own and manage his newly acquired plantation in Alabama, but returned in 1841 to St. Simons Island.

Roswell King Jr.'s past was shrouded in accusations and rumors that injured his reputation. The 1850 census revealed that he controlled three thousand acres and one hundred slaves. He left the Butler estates one last time in 1854. Dying on July 1, 1854 from dysentery and scarlet fever, his grave lies next to Julia's in the Colonial Midway Cemetery at Midway, Georgia.

Barrington King

Barrington King (1798-1866) was the third son of Roswell King. He was an intelligent and successful businessman, who had the most impact on the early growth of the town and its survival after the Civil War. His wise and diverse investments provided funds postwar to reopen one of the textile mills and prevented the town from being lost in history. Barrington's letter to President Andrew Johnson asking for a pardon and restoration of citizenship appears in this book's Appendix, Figures 1-4. Citizenship was a necessity since he was RMC's president and needed to do business in the United States. Unfortunately, as a result of an accident involving a horse, Barrington died in January 1866.

Ralph Brown King

Ralph Brown King (1801-1878) was their fourth son. His first wife was Isabella M. Gibbs, and he sired two children with her. He married his second wife Mildred H. Bronaugh in 1859. Ralph became a New York broker and handled Anna Whistler's financial affairs in the 1850's. He was an intimate friend of Anna Matilda McNeill Whistler, mother of the American artist, James McNeil Whistler. Mildred Bronaugh King was Anna's first cousin.

Ralph was also the nephew of Zephaniah Kingsley Jr. of the Kingsley Plantation in Jacksonville, Florida. Ralph and Isabella's daughter married Anna's son William McNeill Whistler, who was a physician and Confederate soldier. As a Confederate Army surgeon, William was stationed at the Richmond smallpox hospital, Libby Prison, and with Orr's South Carolina Rifles. Ralph survived the war; the last record showed him living in New Orleans.

William King

William King (1804-1884) was Roswell King's sixth son and born on St. Simons Island. He married Sarah E. McLeod from Savannah (1807-1891) and sired four children. He lived in nearby Marietta during the Civil War.

In September 1864, General Sherman's Federal forces surrounded Atlanta, and waited for its surrender. William King was asked to be the intermediary between General William Tecumseh Sherman and Governor Joseph Emerson Brown. Sherman chose William King, a prominent Southerner with an honest reputation, to take a proposal to Brown. Sherman offered to terminate the siege on Atlanta and treat kindly the civilian population, if Brown agreed to secede Georgia from the Confederacy. The proposal was not accepted by the Confederate authorities.

As General W.T. Sherman campaigned through northern Georgia, William informed Barrington King and Reverend Pratt of the Union Army's activities; he warned them of approaching troop movement toward Roswell. William King's diary of July through September 1864 gave detailed interactions with Generals Thomas, McArthur, and McCook, commanders of Union troops occupying Marietta. It included the arrest, capture, and escape of James R. King by Union troops in July 1864. King would be captured again one month later. William talked about the arrest of the Roswell mill workers who were imprisoned and waiting for transport north. The diary ends with details about the various robberies, grave desecrations by soldiers, and specifics about the assault on Atlanta. William King survived the war; he died in 1884 at age 79 from pneumonia. He was buried in Marietta's Citizen (City) Cemetery.

Elizabeth Barrington King

Elizabeth Barrington King (Hand) (1808-1883) was the ninth child of Roswell King. She married Bayard E. Hand and settled in Sunbury near Midway, Georgia.

The parents of Bayard E. Hand (Sr.), Aaron and Tamar Hand, were from New York State. Aaron Hand was a lumber merchant originally from New Milford, Connecticut, and later Kingsbury, New York. He married Tamar Platt of Albany, who was the sister of Anna Platt. Anna Platt married George King, who was Roswell King's brother.

Aaron and Tamar's son, Bayard E. Hand, moved to Midway, Georgia, in 1823. He became a lawyer and served as his father's agent for the lumbering business. He was also a bank president. He met Elizabeth King in Darien, and they were married in 1824. Elizabeth and Bayard invested in Roswell's textile mills, thus becoming one of the six founding families. They had eight children, but three children died prior to relocating to Roswell, and one child died in Roswell during the scarlet fever epidemic in 1841.

Bayard Hand suffered from a long history of dyspepsia and became seriously ill; he possibly had stomach cancer. He died at home in Sunbury on October 4, 1838. Elizabeth moved to Roswell and into her new home, Primrose Cottage, after his death.

Catherine Barrington King

Catherine Barrington King (Pratt) (1810-1894) was the last child born to Roswell King in Darien, Georgia. She married the Reverend Nathaniel Alpheus Pratt in 1830. She was an educated woman for those times, since Catherine attended Sarah Pierce's Female Academy in Litchfield, Connecticut.

Reverend Pratt served as minister to the Darien Presbyterian Church. Roswell King invited Reverend Pratt to move to Roswell, invest in the mill, and become the first minister of the new church. (Roswell's Presbyterian Church was started in Elizabeth Hand's home, Primrose Cottage).

The Pratts raised ten children including three sons who served in the Confederate Army. During the Union occupation, the Pratts were the only founding family members who remained in Roswell. Reverend Pratt documented the activities that occurred during the Union occupation sending letters and keeping journals. Catherine and Nathaniel Pratt were buried in the Presbyterian Church Cemetery.

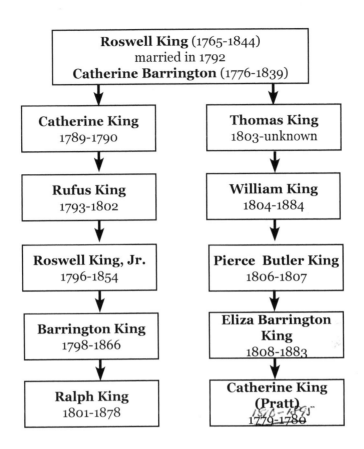

Roswell King (1765-1844)
married in 1792
Catherine Barrington (1776-1839)

Catherine King
1789-1790

Thomas King
1803-unknown

Rufus King
1793-1802

William King
1804-1884

Roswell King, Jr.
1796-1854

Pierce Butler King
1806-1807

Barrington King
1798-1866

Eliza Barrington
King
1808-1883

Ralph King
1801-1878

Catherine King
(Pratt)
1779-1780

King / Hand / Bayard Roots

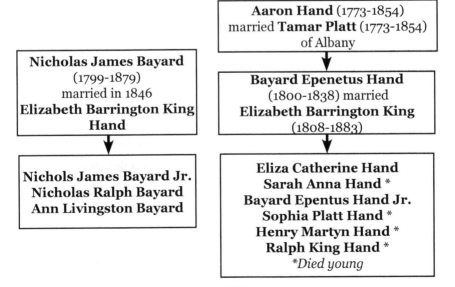

Aaron Hand (1773-1854)
married Tamar Platt (1773-1854)
of Albany

Nicholas James Bayard
(1799-1879)
married in 1846
Elizabeth Barrington King
Hand

Bayard Epenetus Hand
(1800-1838) married
Elizabeth Barrington King
(1808-1883)

Nichols James Bayard Jr.
Nicholas Ralph Bayard
Ann Livingston Bayard

Eliza Catherine Hand
Sarah Anna Hand *
Bayard Epentus Hand Jr.
Sophia Platt Hand *
Henry Martyn Hand *
Ralph King Hand *
*Died young

C. Barrington King Family...The Royal Family

With the death of Roswell King in 1844, Barrington King's family became the focus of Roswell's business and social life. Barrington and Catherine Nephew King bore twelve children; two children died of scarlet fever in 1841, and the last child, a female, died as an infant.

Six of their sons fought for the Confederacy. The other two, one a minister and the other a physician, served the cause by caring for the soldiers. Barrington's RMC aided the cause by donating certain mill products to the Confederacy. The King family descendants, who lived at Barrington Hall, kept the RMC stockholders' minutes and ledgers of the Ivy Mills. Some records were eventually lost in a fire, but those that remained left a picture of the companies' struggles and achievements.

The following are highlights about each member of "The Royal Family."

Barrington and Catherine King

Barrington King (the third son of Roswell King) and Catherine Margaret Esther Nephew King bore twelve children. She was the daughter of a Revolutionary War soldier, James Nephew and his wife, Mary Magdalene Gignilliat. Catherine was born on her father's cotton plantation, Manchester, in McIntosh County near Baisden's Bluff. James also owned Ceylon Plantation. Some of the King children were born on St. Simons Island, while others were born in Chatham, Liberty, and McIntosh counties, Georgia.

Barrington was the first president of Roswell Manufacturing Company (RMC) and the driving force for the building of the Colony and mills along with his father. He chose the site for Barrington Hall built in 1842. Two of their sons died while fighting for the Confederacy (Thomas and Barrington Simeral King).

Barrington remained president of RMC for twenty-seven years until his death, as a result of an accident with his horse in 1866. The RMC stockholders honored him by erecting the monument that sits on his grave in the Presbyterian Cemetery.

Children of Barrington and Catherine King
Charles Barrington

(Reverend) Charles Barrington (1824-1880) married Anna Wylly Habersham (1827-1915); they had nine children. He matriculated from Franklin College (University of Georgia), and the Seminary College at Princeton as a Presbyterian minister. He served churches in Savannah and Columbus, Georgia, for more than forty years. During the Union occupation of Roswell, Barrington and Catherine fled to Charles' home in Savannah. Charles and Anna are buried in Laurel Grove Cemetery in Savannah.

William Nephew King

(Dr.) William Nephew King (1825-1894) married Virginia Way and sired two children. They mostly lived in Savannah, Georgia. He cared for his wounded brothers and other soldiers during the Civil War. He was a well-known and respected doctor in Roswell.

In 1879, William and his wife moved to New York City, where she died. In New York, William married Fanny De Camp and sired two more children. He decided to further specialize and graduated from the New York College of Physicians and Surgeons. He also studied surgery in Paris for three years and returned to New York City, where he specialized in diseases of children and women.

James Roswell King

James Roswell King (1827-1897) married Fanny Hillhouse Prince (1823-1881). He owned and lived in Holly Hill, an antebellum house once owned by Robert Adams Lewis in Roswell. James and Fanny had ten children. James managed Ivy Mills and organized the Roswell Battalion cavalry with his brother Thomas. James later joined the Confederate Army as captain and performed railroad construction work for the Confederacy. He led the Roswell Battalion when ordered to burn Roswell's bridge in July 1864; he was captured in August 1864, by Federal forces.

After Fanny's death, James married his cousin Meta Lewis and moved to Atlanta. James and Fanny are buried in the King's plot at the Presbyterian Church Cemetery.

Thomas E. King

Thomas Edward King (1829-1863) married Marie Reid Clemons in 1854, and sired three children. They rented Bulloch Hall after Martha Bulloch moved to New York City to live with her daughter, Mittie. He did his patriotic duty by joining the Confederate Army early in 1861, and fought at the First Battle of Manassas, where he was seriously wounded. He was killed at the Battle of Chickamauga in 1863, while serving on Brig. General Preston Smith's staff. His grave lies in Roswell's Presbyterian Church Cemetery. Thomas's widow, Marie King, fled from the Federal forces to Macon, while living at Bulloch Hall.

Nephew and Susan King

Nephew King (1830-1841) died along with his sister, Susan Jones King (1832-1841), during a scarlet fever epidemic that attacked the Colony of Roswell's children. They were buried in Founders Cemetery, later their graves were moved to the Presbyterian Church Cemetery.

Barrington Simeral King

Barrington Simeral King (1833-1865) married Sarah Elizabeth "Bessie" Macleod from Missouri and sired three children. He was a homeopathic physician who practiced in Atlanta for a time. He moved his family to Columbia, South Carolina, to start a new medical practice in 1860. When the war broke out, he joined Cobb's Legion as a colonel and moved his family to Virginia, when his unit was called to fight.

Colonel King died from a wound that severed an artery in his leg, while leading a charge against Kilpatrick's camp at Aversboro, North Carolina. In February 1866, King's body was shipped home and reburied in the Presbyterian Cemetery.

Col. Barrington S. King's grave marker, author's photograph

Ralph Browne King

Ralph Browne King (1835-1900) married Florence Stilwell of New York. Ralph became a lieutenant under General W. J. Hardee and a member of the Chatham County Artillery during the war. He sustained a debilitating wound, which never completely healed. He moved to New York City after the war and worked for Tiffany's.

Catherine Evelyn King

Catherine Evelyn "Eva" King Baker (1837-1923) married the Reverend William Elliott Baker in 1856. William graduated from Princeton in 1850. He attended Columbia Seminary, South Carolina, and returned to Princeton to complete seminary training in 1854. Reverend Baker traveled to Sacramento, California, to start the Westminster Presbyterian Church in 1856. He returned to marry Eva in Georgia, before they both traveled back to California. Eva insisted on returning to Roswell and delivered their first child at Barrington Hall.

William was offered and accepted the ministry post at the First Presbyterian Church in Staunton, Virginia. Reverend Wilson, who was the father of future President Woodrow Wilson, previously held the post. Eva and William raised their seven children throughout the Civil War at Staunton. Today, that Virginia home is showcased to the public as the birthplace of President Woodrow Wilson.

In 1883, William and Eva Baker moved their family into Barrington Hall to live with Eva's elderly mother, Catherine Barrington King. After Mrs. King's death, Eva and William purchased Barrington Hall from the estate. When William died, Eva remained at Barrington Hall until her death in 1924.

Their oldest son, William Elliott, went to Chicago to learn the wholesale grocery business and became interested in the coffee industry. He and his brother migrated to Minneapolis. They started a coffee empire, *Baker and Company* in 1881; the company became successful and had several sales offices in New York, Chicago, and Saint Louis. During WWI, the company began to make soluble or instant coffee, similar to that made by the George Washington Company that first produced this new product. By 1944, Baker & Company was sold to Hygrade Foods.

Joseph Henry King

Joseph Henry King (1839-1917) married Nellie Palmer Stubbs. Prior to the secession of Georgia from the Union, he traveled to Fort Pulaski and joined the Confederate Army as a private. He served under the command of General Bartow and General Joseph Johnston. During the First Battle of Manassas, Joseph was seriously wounded in the hip, leg, and hand; he never fully recovered from his wounds.

Once the war ended, Joseph built a popular rest site on the Florida Intracoastal Waterway called *Eldorado*. Years later, after his death in 1928, almost all of his descendants drowned in Lake Okeechobee from a large tidal surge during the great category 4 hurricane of 1928. The Joseph King bloodline ended.

Clifford Alonzo King

Clifford Alonzo King (1842-1911) married Eliza Hardee (b. 1844) during the Civil War. He was made a captain in the Confederate Army serving under General W. J. Hardee, Eliza's uncle. Clifford and Eliza had seven children; after her death he married a woman named Virginia. They eventually moved to Texas to grow cotton; soon he had so much financial misfortune that he had to declare bankruptcy.

Later, Clifford moved his family to Colorado Springs and bought a share in a mining business. His misfortunes continued when he was lowered by rope to explore a mine and the rope broke. Clifford plunged to his death and was buried in Idaho Springs, Colorado. One of his sons, John Hardee King, performed in Vaudeville. Clifford's two granddaughters, Mamie and Jane, performed on a Broadway stage.

The Royal Family

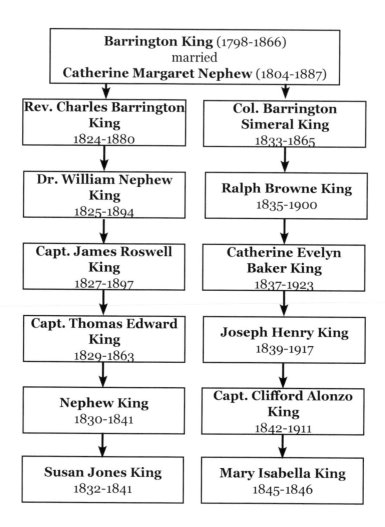

Barrington King (1798-1866)
married
Catherine Margaret Nephew (1804-1887)

Rev. Charles Barrington King
1824-1880

Col. Barrington Simeral King
1833-1865

Dr. William Nephew King
1825-1894

Ralph Browne King
1835-1900

Capt. James Roswell King
1827-1897

Catherine Evelyn Baker King
1837-1923

Capt. Thomas Edward King
1829-1863

Joseph Henry King
1839-1917

Nephew King
1830-1841

Capt. Clifford Alonzo King
1842-1911

Susan Jones King
1832-1841

Mary Isabella King
1845-1846

King Descendants

Barrington and Catherine Margaret King have more than 1,350 descendants according to a 2004 family reunion held at Barrington Hall. The last private owners of Barrington Hall, Sarah Winner and Les Hunter, her husband, hosted the event.

D. Bulloch Family...
Political Giants Run In The Family

The American Bulloch family traces their Scottish heritage back to the MacDonald clan. The Bulloch branch of Georgia made a significant impact on our fledgling country's survival. The Bullochs claim famous personages from Archibald Bulloch, President of Georgia's Provincial Congress, to Theodore "Rough Rider" Roosevelt, the 26th President of the United States. There were other notables related to this family including a Confederate Naval Agent, Continental Army generals, a Georgia Senator, WWI and WWII heroes, a First Lady, and the first United States delegate to the United Nations.

First Bulloch in The English Colonies, James Bulloch

James Balloch (Bulloch) was born in 1701 in Glasgow, Scotland. His parentage remains unknown to this day, but it can be narrowed to one of two brothers, James and William Balloch. William Balloch was chamberlain to King David II and he married Jean Reid; James Balloch married Margaret Leckie. Either pair could have fathered James. (During the 17th century, the name changed from Balloch to Bulloch).

James Bulloch (1701-1781) became a minister and a scholar of Latin and Greek. He came to the British colonies in 1728 to begin his new life as a Charles Town (Charleston) merchant in the Carolinas. One year later, James married Jean Stobo and sired three children; she brought PonPon Plantation to the marriage. One of their sons was Archibald Bulloch, grandfather of James Stephens Bulloch, a founder of Roswell.

Reverend James experienced much tragedy in his life; he married and was widowed four times. James's second wife was Anne Barker Skipper Ferguson. Anne was the widow of James

Ferguson; she previously had been married to and was a widow of William Skipper.

James' third wife, Anne Cuthbert Graham, brought Mulberry Grove Plantation to the marriage. Anne was previously married to Dr. Patrick Graham, who made Mulberry Grove a thriving rice plantation near the Savannah River. Mulberry Grove Plantation was a large productive estate, but after six years, James sold it. The estate experienced several owners until it became the property of John Graham, Lt. Governor of the Province of Georgia. Georgia patriots confiscated Mulberry Grove Plantation during the Revolutionary War from John Graham because of his Troy allegiance. The plantation was given to Major General Nathaniel Green for his part in rescuing Georgia from the British during the Revolutionary War.

Lastly, James married Mary Jones who had inherited Wormsloe Plantation from her father. Noble Jones was one of the original settlers who came to Georgia Colony with General Oglethorpe. Mary Jones was a sister of Dr. Noble Wimberly Jones, physician, statesman, and patriot during the War for Independence. Wormsloe Plantation in Savannah became Reverend James Bulloch's property when he married Mary Jones; she died without bearing any children.

Reverend James Bulloch held many positions during his life. He was the King's Justice of the Peace for Colleton County, South Carolina in 1735, Special Agent to the Creeks in 1740, member of the South Carolina Colonial Assembly (Legislature) in 1754, Georgia Justice for Christ Church Parish in 1767, and member of the Provincial Congress in 1775. When James died in 1780, he was buried beneath ancient moss-veiled live oaks at Wormsloe Plantation.

Archibald Bulloch....Presidential Material

The Reverend James Bulloch and Jean Stobo's son, Archibald Bulloch (1731-1777) was born in Charles Town, and became a planter while living in the Carolinas. He married Mary DeVeaux (1748-1818) whose parents were Anne Fairchild and Judge James DeVeaux. They were descendants of French Huguenots, who fled from persecution to the Carolinas during the 17th century.

Archibald and Mary bore three sons and one daughter named James, Jane, William Berringer, and Archibald Stobo. Archibald Bulloch and Mary moved their family to Savannah in 1764. Their daughter, Jane Bulloch, married James B. Maxwell of the aristocratic Maxwell family. Their oldest son, James Bulloch (1765) was named for his grandfather.

Archibald (1731) was a merchant and invested in the first regular shipping company to New York City and the West Indies. Bulloch was an outspoken radical in his family; he was viewed by the public as a courageous leader, statesman, and soldier prior to the Revolutionary War.

On January 17, 1775, the Georgia Assembly was called to order by Governor James Wright. They had to decide whether to join the Continental Association, which voted to ban trade with Britain. Many Georgians were not supporters of the patriotic cause that burned so brightly in New England. The Upper and Lower Houses discussed preserving American rights as British subjects.

The Georgia Provincial Congress eventually did adopt the articles passed by the First Continental Congress with a few exceptions dealing with trade and Britain. They also elected five delegates to the Second Continental Congress and agreed Georgia would help to defray expenses in the defense of those rights.

Archibald Bulloch was elected Speaker of the Royal Assembly of Georgia and President of the Provincial Congress in 1775 and President of the Executive Council.

In Philadelphia on May 10, 1775, the Second Continental Congress did not feel that Georgia had acted in good faith regarding trade with Britain and her trading partners. The Continental Congress wanted to cut off trade with the youngest colony, Georgia; on the day they were meeting, disturbing news came about Breed's Hill. This resulted in more Georgians supporting the Continental Congress' stance against Great Britain. A group that was encouraging Georgia toward open revolt was the Council of Safety, whose leader was Archibald Bulloch. On July 6, 1775, the Second Georgia Provincial Congress accepted the provisions of the Continental Congress.

The following day, July 7th, the Second Georgia Provincial Congress elected five men to represent the colony at the Second Continental Congress; they included John Zubly, John Houstoun, Archibald Bulloch, Noble W. Jones, and Lyman Hall.

Archibald Bulloch was chosen to command Georgia troops and defend Georgia from the British. Commander-in-chief Colonel Bulloch led the Georgia militia on March 25, 1776, in the defense of Savannah against the British in the Tybee Island expedition and the Battle of the Rice Boats.

Georgia sent three delegates in July 1776, to the Philadelphia convention to sign the Declaration of Independence. They were Lyman Hall, George Walton, and Button Gwinnett. Bulloch stayed in Georgia but was given the honor to publicly read the document in 1777 to the Savannah residents. Archibald suddenly died a mysterious death in February 1777; some writings suggest he was poisoned but this is only speculative. He was buried in Savannah's Colonial Park Cemetery. Archibald was the great-great-grandfather of President Theodore Roosevelt, who knowingly followed in Archibald's famous political and military footsteps.

Bulloch Baldernoch Scottish Roots

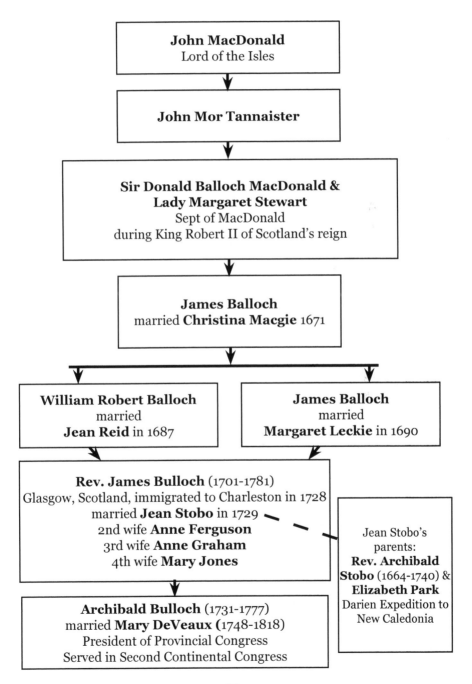

John MacDonald
Lord of the Isles

John Mor Tannaister

**Sir Donald Balloch MacDonald &
Lady Margaret Stewart**
Sept of MacDonald
during King Robert II of Scotland's reign

James Balloch
married **Christina Macgie** 1671

William Robert Balloch
married
Jean Reid in 1687

James Balloch
married
Margaret Leckie in 1690

Rev. James Bulloch (1701-1781)
Glasgow, Scotland, immigrated to Charleston in 1728
married **Jean Stobo** in 1729
2nd wife **Anne Ferguson**
3rd wife **Anne Graham**
4th wife **Mary Jones**

Jean Stobo's
parents:
**Rev. Archibald
Stobo** (1664-1740) &
Elizabeth Park
Darien Expedition to
New Caledonia

Archibald Bulloch (1731-1777)
married **Mary DeVeaux** (1748-1818)
President of Provincial Congress
Served in Second Continental Congress

Children of Archibald Bulloch
& Mary DeVeaux

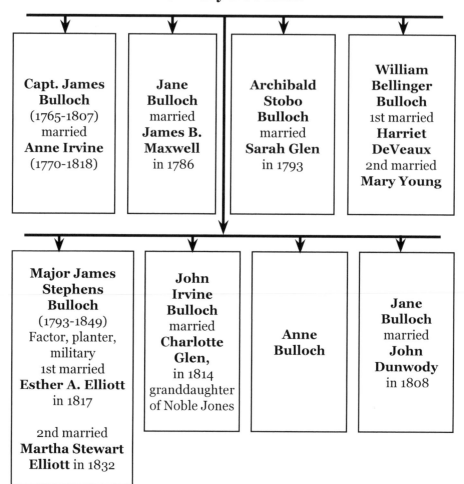

Capt. James Bulloch (1765-1807) married Anne Irvine (1770-1818)	Jane Bulloch married James B. Maxwell in 1786	Archibald Stobo Bulloch married Sarah Glen in 1793	William Bellinger Bulloch 1st married Harriet DeVeaux 2nd married Mary Young

Major James Stephens Bulloch (1793-1849) Factor, planter, military 1st married Esther A. Elliott in 1817 2nd married Martha Stewart Elliott in 1832	John Irvine Bulloch married Charlotte Glen, in 1814 granddaughter of Noble Jones	Anne Bulloch	Jane Bulloch married John Dunwody in 1808

Irvine Family Roots
Dumfries / Aberdeen Scotland

Dr. John Irvine married **Ann Elizabeth Baille**
of Dunone Plantation.
He practiced medicine in Sunbury &
Savannah, founder of Georgia Medical Society

Anne Irvine married **Capt. James Bulloch** (1765-1807)
grandparents of **Martha *Mittie* Bulloch Roosevelt**

(Captain) James Bulloch....Revolutionary War Patriot

(Captain) James Bulloch, (1765-1806) was named for his grandfather and married Anne Irvine in 1786 (1748-1818). Anne Irvine was the daughter of Dr. John Irvine who migrated from Dumfrieshire, Scotland, near Aberdeen to Georgia in 1765. He practiced medicine in Sunbury and Savannah. Dr. Irvine married Ann Elizabeth Baille of Plantation Duone; they claimed to be related to King Robert Bruce of Scotland.

(Captain) James Bulloch became a Captain in the Continental Army during the Revolutionary War. In 1778 when he was thirteen, the British captured Savannah, and he had to flee to Virginia. He joined the Virginia State Garrison between 1778 and 1780; James rapidly advanced to the rank of captain by the age of seventeen. After the British evacuated Savannah, James returned home and worked as Clerk of the Courts of Georgia. At that time, Captain Bulloch became active in the Georgia Troops to repel Indian uprisings. He served as captain of the East Savannah Company, 1st Regiment, Georgia Militia from 1786-1789. Captain James Bulloch enjoyed membership in the prestigious Society of Cincinnati in Georgia. Captain James Bulloch died in 1807.

Captain James and Anne Bulloch bore four children; they included John Irvine, Jane, James Stephens, and Anne. They often brought their children to visit Dr. and Mrs. Irvine (Anne's parents) in Sunbury, Georgia. During the many visits to the Irvine home in Sunbury, Jane Bulloch met Dr. James Dunwody's son, John Dunwody, and they were eventually married. Jane and John Dunwody became one of the founding families of Roswell.

Jane (Bulloch) Dunwody was a friend of John Dunwody's sister, Esther. Esther and her husband, John Elliott, owned Laurel View Plantation at Sunbury. John and Esther Elliott's daughter, (Hester) Esther Amarinthia Elliott, was a childhood friend of (Major) James Stephens Bulloch.

(Major) James Stephens Bulloch.....
Grandfather of a President

(Major) James Stephens Bulloch married John Elliott's daughter Hester (Esther) Amarinthia Elliott (his childhood friend) on December 31, 1817, at Midway Church. They bore two children, but only one son survived, James Dunwody Bulloch.

(Major) James Stephens Bulloch (1793-1849) was a factor, planter, and soldier from Savannah. He held offices of bank director and director and small investor in a ship building company. That company built the first steamship to cross the Atlantic Ocean, the *Savannah*. The *Savannah* was not a commercial success as a steamship; it was converted back into a sailing ship shortly after returning from Europe. The ship was wrecked off the coast of Long Island, New York, in 1821. No other American-owned steamship would cross the Atlantic for almost thirty years after the *Savannah's* pioneering voyage.

(Major) James Bulloch served as an ensign in the Georgia Militia during the War of 1812, with the 60th Battalion, 1st Regiment, Georgia Militia. This battalion was comprised of Savannah Volunteer Guards, the Republican Blues, and other Savannah companies; they did not see any actual fighting around Savannah.

(Major) James Bulloch became a commissioned captain in July of 1816 and later elected to the rank of major on August 9, 1817. He served as the commander of the 3rd Beat Company, also called the Courthouse Company. He joined the Chatham Artillery and was elected first lieutenant on February 4, 1826.

James' wife, Hester, died in Savannah, in 1831, after a prolonged illness. James and his eight-year-old son moved into Martha Stewart Elliott's (his step mother-in-law) home. One year later, James and Martha were married on May 8, 1832.

A daughter, Anna Bulloch, was born to James and Martha in 1833. By 1835, they moved to Connecticut in order to place young James Dunwody Bulloch into the Hartford Academy. Another daughter was born to Martha and James named Martha (Mittie), while living in Connecticut. Upon returning to Savannah, James was offered a position with Roswell King's mill as a company stockholder and director. The Bullochs agreed to participate in this new adventure in north Georgia.

In the spring of 1838, Major James S. Bulloch, Martha Stewart Elliott Bulloch, six children, and six slaves began the long journey from Savannah to the Colony of Roswell on the Hightower Indian Trail. Upon arrival in Roswell, the Bullochs selected a ten-acre plot high on a ridge in the village. Willis Ball was selected to build the Greek Revival house named Bulloch Hall. While the house was under construction, the Bulloch family lived in an abandoned Cherokee farmhouse near present day Martin's Landing. The family moved into their completed house about 1839.

In 1838, Charles Irvine Bulloch was born to the Bullochs. In 1841, a scarlet fever epidemic attacked the Roswell children. Charles was the first child to die and was buried in the Founders Cemetery on a knoll above the mill village. The epidemic killed other Roswell children including Ralph King Hand, two Barrington King children, and several millworkers' children.

Irvine Stephens Bulloch, born at Bulloch Hall in June 1842, was the full brother of Mittie Bulloch. He married Ella Sears (1849-1911) an American who was living in Liverpool after the Civil War. He fought for the Confederate Navy; in 1861 he was a midshipman on the CSS *Nashville*. Later, he became the youngest officer on the CSS *Alabama* during its many attacks on the Union's blockade and merchant marine vessels. Known for his excellent navigational skills, he was chosen as the sailing master on the CSS *Shenandoah*, surrendering the ship to the British in Liverpool in 1865. Irvine died of Bright's disease and a cerebral hemorrhage in Selby Town, Wales. He was buried at Toxteth Park Cemetery, Liverpool, England.

Several major changes happened in Martha's life over the next several years. Sadness came to the Bulloch family with the death of Georgia Amanda Elliott (Martha's daughter) in 1848; she was buried in Founders Cemetery. The marriage of Susan Elliott, Martha's daughter, to (Dr.) Hilborne West of Philadelphia was held at Bulloch Hall in 1849. Major James Bulloch suddenly suffered a stroke while teaching Sunday school at the Presbyterian Church; he died on February 18, 1849 and was buried in the Founders Cemetery near his son, Charles Irvine and step-daughter Georgia Elliott.

Young Theodore Roosevelt (Sr.) of New York City met Mittie Bulloch, Martha and James' daughter, possibly in February of 1851 in Roswell. Two years passed, and Theodore became reacquainted with Mittie Bulloch at her sister's home in Philadelphia. They married in 1853 at Bulloch Hall.

(Captain) James Dunwody Bulloch...
Confederate Naval Agent

(Captain) James Dunwody Bulloch (1823-1901), son of Major James S. Bulloch and Hester Amarinthia Elliott, visited his father and stepmother, Martha, in Roswell, but he never lived at Bulloch Hall. Captain Bulloch married Elizabeth Caskie of Richmond, Virginia, in 1851. Bulloch served in the United States Navy for fifteen years, he resigned his commission to join a private shipping company in 1854.

After Elizabeth's death from tuberculosis, he married Harriott Cross Foster of Baton Rouge, Louisiana, in 1857, and

James Stephens Bulloch Family

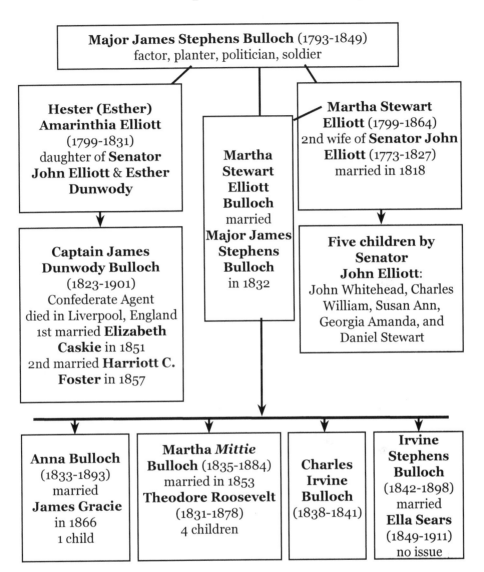

Major James Stephens Bulloch (1793-1849)
factor, planter, politician, soldier

Hester (Esther) Amarinthia Elliott (1799-1831) daughter of **Senator John Elliott** & **Esther Dunwody**

Martha Stewart Elliott Bulloch married Major James Stephens Bulloch in 1832

Martha Stewart Elliott (1799-1864) 2nd wife of **Senator John Elliott** (1773-1827) married in 1818

Captain James Dunwody Bulloch (1823-1901) Confederate Agent died in Liverpool, England 1st married **Elizabeth Caskie** in 1851 2nd married **Harriott C. Foster** in 1857

Five children by Senator John Elliott: John Whitehead, Charles William, Susan Ann, Georgia Amanda, and Daniel Stewart

Anna Bulloch (1833-1893) married **James Gracie** in 1866 1 child

Martha *Mittie* Bulloch (1835-1884) married in 1853 **Theodore Roosevelt** (1831-1878) 4 children

Charles Irvine Bulloch (1838-1841)

Irvine Stephens Bulloch (1842-1898) married **Ella Sears** (1849-1911) no issue

sired five children. The children were James Jr., Jessie Hart, Henry, Stuart Elliott, and Martha Louise.

In April 1861, he commanded a United States Mail steamer and traveled between New York City; Havana, Cuba; and New Orleans; while in New Orleans in 1861, Captain James D. Bulloch offered to assist the Confederacy. He met with Secretary of the Navy, Stephen Mallory, in Montgomery, Alabama. Captain

Bulloch was assigned the role of a Naval Agent for the Confederacy. He traveled to Liverpool, England, to oversee the funding and building of several cruisers for the Confederacy. These ships sailed in the Atlantic, Pacific, and Indian Oceans.

Britain was officially neutral during the American Civil War, but private and public sentiment favored the Confederacy. Britain was also willing to buy all the cotton that could be smuggled past the Union blockade, the only real source of Confederate revenue. Captain Bulloch's job was to establish a relationship with the shipping firm of Fraser, Trenholm, & Company and to buy and sell Confederate cotton. Bulloch arranged for cotton to be converted to hard currency, which was used to purchase war materiel such as arms, ammunition, uniforms, and naval supplies for the Confederacy.

He orchestrated the construction of the CSS *Florida* and the CSS *Alabama*. Both cruisers preyed on the Union's Merchant Marine fleet. James' younger half-brother, Irvine S. Bulloch, served in the Confederate States Navy on the CSS *Alabama*. Later Irvine sailed on the CSS *Shenandoah*; the cruiser fired the last shots of the war on June 28, 1865, during a raid on American whalers in the Bering Sea.

There are many ships and cruisers that were used in the Confederate Navy as a result of Captain Bulloch's efforts, but they are too numerous to list here. (See Wilson and MacKay book for a complete listing).

After the war, James was not included in the general amnesty; he and Irvine became British citizens and chose to live in England. They made many trips back to the United States after the war as British subjects. Captain Bulloch continued to live with his family in Liverpool, England.

Theodore Roosevelt (Jr.) visited his Uncle Jimmie in England many times and gathered research about War of 1812 naval tactics and strategies. Theodore's book, written with the details that James related, remains the most authoritative account of the war.

Captain James D. Bulloch died from rectal cancer and heart failure in 1901; he was buried at Toxteth Cemetery Park, Liverpool, England. Written on his memorial stone is the following: *An American by Birth, an Englishman by Choice.*

Captain James Dunwody Bulloch Lineage

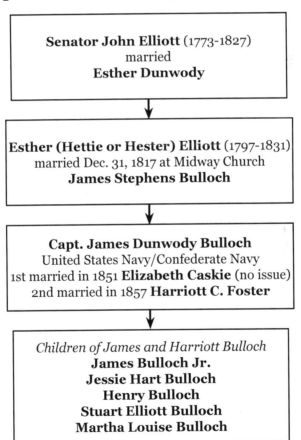

Senator John Elliott (1773-1827)
married
Esther Dunwody

Esther (Hettie or Hester) Elliott (1797-1831)
married Dec. 31, 1817 at Midway Church
James Stephens Bulloch

Capt. James Dunwody Bulloch
United States Navy/Confederate Navy
1st married in 1851 Elizabeth Caskie (no issue)
2nd married in 1857 Harriott C. Foster

Children of James and Harriott Bulloch
James Bulloch Jr.
Jessie Hart Bulloch
Henry Bulloch
Stuart Elliott Bulloch
Martha Louise Bulloch

E. Stewarts and Elliotts Merge Families
Daniel Stewart...Brave Soldier and Patriot

The first Stewarts who settled in Georgia came from South Carolina; they chose to live in the Sunbury, Darien, and Midway regions in 1752. They were English and Scottish Presbyterians who migrated south from Massachusetts and Connecticut.

The Stewarts established Tranquil Plantation on the New Port River and were among those pioneers who established the Midway Church. Susannah Bacon and John Stewart had a son, Daniel Stewart (1761-1829) in Liberty County. When Daniel was five years old, his mother died and his father married Sarah Nickols in 1769. John Stewart became a militia officer in the War for Independence and died in 1776.

His son, Daniel enlisted that same year in the Georgia militia at the age of fifteen under Colonel John Baker of Liberty County. After fighting for two years, Daniel was wounded in 1778 and captured by the British near Charles Town. He was placed aboard a British prison ship in the harbor. Miraculously, he was able to escape by swimming to shore and later returned to his unit. As he hid in South Carolina, he met his first wife-to-be, Martha Pender. Martha died during childbirth one year after their wedding; their son John, named for his grandfather was born on March 21, 1784.

By the age of twenty-two, Daniel was made a colonel of a cavalry brigade, the Minutemen of Georgia. Once the war ended, he established Cedar Hill Plantation in Liberty County. The British destroyed the Georgia countryside and burned Midway Church during the War for Independence. Fourteen years later in 1792, John Elliott, John Dunwody, and Daniel Stewart rebuilt the church.

Daniel's second marriage was to Sarah Susannah Oswald in 1785; Daniel sent for John, who was living with relatives in

South Carolina. Their family members were John (1787-1823), Mary (1788-1823), Daniel McLachlan (1791-1848), and Martha (1799-1864), who became the mother of Mittie Bulloch. Daniel continued to serve the public as a state representative from 1785-1787, a sheriff for Liberty County from1795 to 1797, and state senator from 1802 to 1811.

When Daniel's second wife died in 1807, he married Sarah Hines Lewis two years later. They had two more daughters. Both daughters died in their teens.

In 1809, he commanded a cavalry brigade to fight Creek Indians along the Georgia frontier. During the War of 1812, Daniel was promoted to brigadier-general of the Georgia Militia He died at his Cedar Hill Plantation near Sunbury on May 27, 1829.

In 1915, the United States Congress erected a monument in the Midway Cemetery in honor of Generals Daniel Stewart and James Screven. Fort Stewart was named in his honor. Stewart's inscription reads *Sacred to the memory of Brigadier General Daniel Stewart a gallant soldier in the Revolution and an officer brevetted for bravery in the Indian Wars.*

An Unusual Marriage Involving Stewart and Elliott Families

This is the story of a marriage, which includes the Stewart and Elliott families. It is one filled with romance and intrigue handed down as a tale within the family. The first participant was Martha Stewart (1799-1864), a friend of Hester (Esther) Elliott. Hester was the daughter of John Elliott. Hester's mother died leaving John Elliott a widower with four children. John Elliott was quite taken with Martha (as the tale goes) and asked General Daniel Stewart for Martha's hand in marriage. Martha's father agreed to the marriage, although John Elliott was twenty-six years Martha's senior.

Stewart and Screven Monument, publisher's photograph

The story often told is one where James Stephens Bulloch had first proposed to Martha but she had declined his offer. He then proposed to and married John Elliott's daughter, Hester. There is no historical record of James' proposal, only family lore.

So, Martha married John Elliott in January1818 at Midway Church; she became stepmother to his four children including

Hester, her friend. The children's ages ranged from 23 to 6 years old.

John Elliott was elected to the United States Senate in 1819. The entire family moved to Washington City, where they entered society with numerous balls and parties. The Elliotts traveled between Washington City, his stately Savannah house, and John's Laurel View Plantation. When John's term ended in 1825, the Elliotts returned to Sunbury with more children; another child, Daniel Elliott, was born in Sunbury in 1827.

Senator John Elliott died at the age of fifty-five from dysentery and was buried in Midway Cemetery in 1827. When Martha's father died one year later in 1828, Martha chose to raise the entire family in Savannah.

F. Bullochs and Roosevelts...
A Move to New York City

Mittie Bulloch and her sister, Anna, completed their education at South Carolina Collegiate Institute at Barnhamville, in Columbia, South Carolina. They traveled to visit their sister, Susan Bulloch West, now living in Philadelphia. It was here that Mittie and Mr. Theodore Roosevelt (Sr.) became reacquainted. After writing to each other for some time, Mr. Roosevelt proposed marriage. With Martha's approval, Mittie and Theodore were married in Roswell.

The Roosevelt family was of Dutch descent, whose ancestors were among the founders of New Amsterdam (New York City). They were the blue blood aristocracy of the Victorian age in America. Theodore's parents were Cornelius Van Shaack Roosevelt and Margaret Barnhill Roosevelt.

Theodore was madly in love with Mittie and remained so his entire life. They were married in the dining room of Bulloch

Hall on December 22, 1853; the guests experienced a week long celebration. (Today, the staff and volunteers of Bulloch Hall, in that very same room, annually reenact the wedding). The newlyweds traveled to New York City, where they resided throughout their marriage.

In 1856, Martha Bulloch rented Bulloch Hall to Thomas King, grandson of Roswell King. Martha moved north to Philadelphia to stay with her daughter Susan. Irvine, Martha's son, entered University of Pennsylvania. Later, Martha and Anna were invited to move in with Mittie and Theodore, to help care for the children.

During the war, Martha and Mittie secretively supported the South by sending packages of clothes, soap, etc. through the naval blockade to their friends. They purchased blankets and food for Confederate prisoners held in two of the northern POW camps, Point Lookout and Fort Delaware. Meanwhile, Theodore hired a substitute to fight in the Union Army as his replacement; he served as the allotment commissioner for New York and traveled with the Union forces.

Back home in Georgia, Daniel Stewart (Stuart) Elliott (Martha's son) married Lucy Sorrell of Savannah, the sister of Brig. General Gilbert Moxley Sorrel of Civil War fame. Daniel served as a Confederate soldier for three months but his consumption (tuberculosis) worsened. He died in 1862 in Roswell and was buried in Roswell's Presbyterian Church Cemetery.

Martha was not able to come south to be with Daniel during his last days because of the travel restrictions caused by the war. Sadly, Martha never returned to Roswell; she died before the end of the Civil War on October 30, 1864 and was buried in Brooklyn's Greenwood Cemetery.

Theodore Roosevelt (Jr.) wrote that his grandmother, Martha, was sympathetic to the Southern Confederacy to the day of her demise. In 1905, he visited Roswell to see his mother's beloved home. Eleanor Roosevelt, Martha's granddaughter, also visited Bulloch Hall several times, when she and President Franklin D. Roosevelt were in Warm Springs, Georgia.

I WANT TO KNOW MORE ABOUT:

THE ROOSEVELT CHILDREN OF NEW YORK CITY

Four children were born to Theodore and Mittie. They were Anna (nicknamed Bami) born in 1855, Theodore Jr. in 1858, Elliott in 1860, and finally Corinne in 1861. The children were raised in New York City hearing stories from their mother about her beloved Roswell and the South.

Their father, Theodore, died in 1878 from stomach cancer; this was a terrible blow to Mittie and the children. Six years after Theodore's death, Mittie died unexpectedly from typhoid fever at her son's (Theodore) home. Theodore's wife, Alice Lee, had just given birth to a daughter, but two days later she died from Bright's disease, a serious kidney ailment. Both women died within hours of each other on February 14, 1884 at Theodore's home. The women were buried with a double funeral and laid to rest at Brooklyn's Greenwood Cemetery. Martha Stewart Elliott Bulloch was previously buried in that cemetery in 1864, far from the South she loved.

Theodore entered public life as a New York State Assemblyman. He held many offices including Police Commissioner of New York, Governor of New York, Assistant Secretary of the Navy, and eventually Vice President of the United States. He became the youngest President of the

United States (1901-1909), when President McKinley was assassinated in 1901.

Martha's granddaughter (Elliott Roosevelt's daughter), Eleanor, married Franklin Delano Roosevelt her 5th cousin. He became the 32nd President of the United States serving from 1933-1945.

Eleanor was known as the *First Lady of the World* because of her humanitarian efforts. Eleanor remained active in politics following her husband's death. She became one of the first delegates to the United Nations (UN), and she served as the first chair of the UN Commission on Human Rights. During John F. Kennedy's administration, she chaired the Presidential Commission on the Status of Women.

MITTIE AND THEODORE ROOSEVELT'S GRANDCHILDREN
THEODORE ROOSEVELT JR.'S CHILDREN

Alice Roosevelt Longworth was the family rebel. She campaigned for her brother Ted as he ran for the New York state governorship against Franklin Delano Roosevelt.

Theodore "Ted" Roosevelt (III) was the eldest son and an investment banker. He fought in both World Wars. During World War I, he was gassed and shot in the left kneecap. In World War II, he led and died just after the invasion of Utah Beach on D-Day at age 57, earning the Medal of Honor.

Kermit Roosevelt, graduate of Harvard University, was an adventurer, writer, soldier and businessman. He joined his father on the African safari, and the River of Doubt expedition in Brazil. He served in both World Wars and was prone to depression and alcoholism. He committed suicide in 1943.

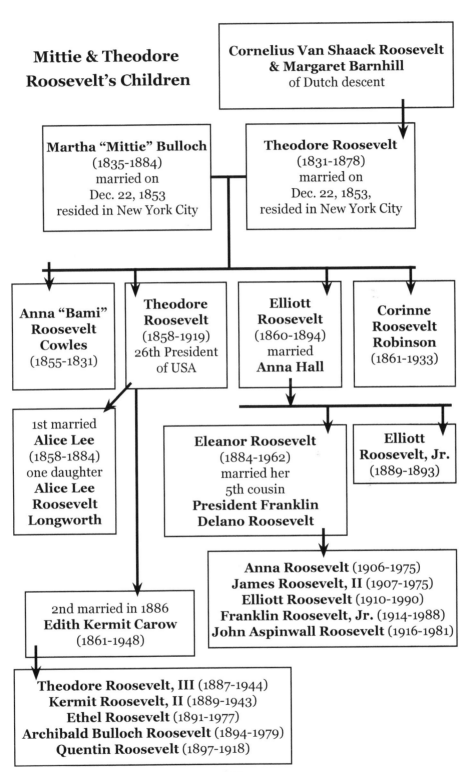

Mittie & Theodore Roosevelt's Children

Cornelius Van Shaack Roosevelt
& Margaret Barnhill
of Dutch descent

Martha "Mittie" Bulloch
(1835-1884)
married on
Dec. 22, 1853
resided in New York City

Theodore Roosevelt
(1831-1878)
married on
Dec. 22, 1853,
resided in New York City

Anna "Bami"
Roosevelt
Cowles
(1855-1831)

Theodore
Roosevelt
(1858-1919)
26th President
of USA

Elliott
Roosevelt
(1860-1894)
married
Anna Hall

Corinne
Roosevelt
Robinson
(1861-1933)

1st married
Alice Lee
(1858-1884)
one daughter
**Alice Lee
Roosevelt
Longworth**

Eleanor Roosevelt
(1884-1962)
married her
5th cousin
**President Franklin
Delano Roosevelt**

Elliott
Roosevelt, Jr.
(1889-1893)

Anna Roosevelt (1906-1975)
James Roosevelt, II (1907-1975)
Elliott Roosevelt (1910-1990)
Franklin Roosevelt, Jr. (1914-1988)
John Aspinwall Roosevelt (1916-1981)

2nd married in 1886
Edith Kermit Carow
(1861-1948)

Theodore Roosevelt, III (1887-1944)
Kermit Roosevelt, II (1889-1943)
Ethel Roosevelt (1891-1977)
Archibald Bulloch Roosevelt (1894-1979)
Quentin Roosevelt (1897-1918)

Ethel Roosevelt Derby, the youngest daughter, married a surgeon. She nursed wounded soldiers during World War I and worked with the Oyster Bay Red Cross.

Archibald Roosevelt was a distinguished Army officer, seriously wounded in WWI and II. He was a businessman and formed the New York investment firm, Roosevelt and Cross.

Quentin Roosevelt dropped out of Harvard to train as an aviator. His plane was shot down during World War I.

ELEANOR ROOSEVELT'S CHILDREN

Anna Roosevelt Dall Boettiger Halsted (1906-1975) was active in both writing and editing. Anna moved into the White House after her separation from Curtis Dall, where she often served as the official hostess. She was present at the Yalta Conference and for many of the major political functions during WWII. She died from throat cancer

James Roosevelt II (1907-1991) attended Harvard and the Boston School of Law. He dropped out of law school and ran a successful insurance company. He became a commissioned Lieutenant Colonel in the Marine Corps, where he earned the Silver Star and retired as a Brigadier General in 1959. He served as a United States Representative from California between 1955-65. He published several memoirs, married four times, and fathered seven children. He died at age 83 in 1991 of Parkinson's disease.

Elliott Roosevelt (1910-1990) became an active member of the Armed Forces during WWII. He enlisted in the US Army Air Corps and served as a pilot and commander. After flying more than three hundred combat missions, he retired as a brigadier general. He married five times, fathered five children, and adopted four others. He died in 1990 at age 80.

Franklin D. Roosevelt Jr. (1914-1988) was the third surviving son. He contracted a serious strep infection in 1936. The infection was successfully treated with the new sulfonamide antibiotics. The press that followed his recovery ushered in a new era of antibiotic acceptance among the public. He married five times and fathered five children. He was involved in politics and the law. He died of throat cancer on his 74th birthday.

John Aspinwall Roosevelt (1916-1981) was the last child born to Eleanor. He served in the US Navy but never campaigned for public office. He retired as vice president of an investment firm before leading various charity organizations. He married twice, and fathered four children before his death in 1981, from heart failure at the age of 65.

G. Dunwody Scottish Lineage...
Pennsylvania's Loss is Georgia's Gain

The American name of Dunwoody has several renditions, all of which are of Scottish origin. They include Dinwithie, Dunwoodie, Dunwody and Dinwiddie.

John Dinwiddie migrated to the American colonies and formed the American Dunwody/Dinwiddie branch, which lived in Virginia and Pennsylvania. Governor Robert Dinwiddie of Virginia played a significant role during colonial America's bid for growth and independence.

John Dunwody migrated from Scotland to the Province of Pennsylvania about 1730. He was an educated man and taught school in Chester County, Pennsylvania. John Dunwody married Susannah Cresswell ten years later, John died in 1776, and Susannah moved to the South with her family. Her children included James, John, and Robert and five sisters.

(Dr.) James Dunwody

(Dr.) James Dunwody, Susannah's first son, came to Georgia and was elected to Georgia's Executive Council in 1776. He lived in Liberty County, where he practiced medicine. He married Esther Dean Splatt, a widow who brought Arcadia Plantation to the marriage. Esther Dunwody, their only daughter, married Senator John Elliott of Liberty County. One of Esther and John's children, Esther (Hester) Elliott married Major James Stephens Bulloch and had one living son, James Dunwody Bulloch.

John Dunwody... A Founder of Roswell

John Dunwody (1786-1858) married Jane Bulloch (1788-1856), sister of (Major) James Stephens Bulloch. They left Arcadia Plantation, located near Midway and Sunbury, for Roswell in 1839. John was the Sunday school superintendent of the Presbyterian Church for seventeen years. They raised six children including three sons, who fought for the Confederacy.

John died after a long-suffering illness on June 6, 1858, his wife had previously died in 1856. Both John and Jane Dunwody were buried in the Founders Cemetery in Roswell. Today their former home is called Mimosa Hall and remains privately owned.

John and Jane Dunwody Children
(Reverend) James B. Dunwody

(Reverend) James B. Dunwody was a Presbyterian minister in South Georgia. He graduated from Yale College and Columbia Theological Seminary. During the Civil War, Dr. Dunwody briefly served as a Chaplain for the Confederacy. He officiated at Mittie and Theodore's wedding on December 22, 1853. He died in South Carolina.

(Lt. Col.) John E. Dunwody Jr.

John Elliott Dunwody Jr., second son of John and Jane Dunwody was born in Hartford, Connecticut. He attended the United States Military Academy between 1838-1846; he resigned to fight in the Mexican War and later served in the Georgia Militia for eight years. He married Elizabeth Clarke Wing.

Lt. Col. Dunwody operated an extensive tannery operation in Lebanon, north of Roswell, prior to the Civil War. The tannery was operating during the arrival of the Union soldiers in Roswell. He died in Atlanta in 1903, and Elizabeth died in 1898; both were buried in Atlanta's Oakland Cemetery.

(Major) Henry Dunwody

(Major) Henry Dunwody married Matilda Elizabeth Maxwell of the Georgia Maxwell aristocracy. Henry met his wife while attending Franklin College in Athens. He became a lawyer and plantation owner in Early County.

During the Civil War, he was appointed captain of the 51st Georgia Infantry at Blakely, Early County, on March 4, 1862. Captain Henry saw little action during the regiment's first encounter at the battle of Seccessionville, South Carolina, on June 16th. The 51st was ordered to Virginia where they fought at South Mountain, Sharpsburg, Fredericksburg, and the Chancellorsville campaign in 1863. Henry was promoted to Major on May 2, 1863 prior to marching to Pennsylvania. Major Henry Dunwody was mortally wounded during the Battle of the Wheatfield in Gettysburg, July 1863. His body was shipped to Roswell for burial.

Tragedy continued for Matilda, all three of her children died between 1866 and 1875. Matilda moved to Savannah to work as a matron in a Savannah hospital. There are no descendants left in this line. The entire family was buried in Roswell's Presbyterian Church Cemetery.

(Dr.) William Elliott Dunwody

Dr. William Elliott Dunwody was born at Cedar Hill Plantation in Liberty County, Georgia. He graduated from the Medical Department of New York in 1845, and practiced medicine in Roswell, Marietta, and Macon. William married Ruth Ann Atwood, daughter of Henry S. Atwood, a Darien manufacturer. Dr. William Dunwody died in Macon in 1891 and was buried at Riverside Cemetery.

(Major) Charles A. Dunwody

(Major) Charles A. Dunwody was born in Liberty County in 1828. He graduated from Franklin College in Athens, Georgia. In 1852, he married Ellen J. Rice, daughter of Honorable William Rice and Rosaline Jackson of Charleston. He owned a shoe manufacturing company in Roswell.

When the Civil War broke out, he enlisted in the Roswell Guard (Georgia's 7th Infantry), and later joined the Roswell Battalion as a private. In 1861, the Roswell Battalion became part of Longstreet's Corps and fought with General Bee's group at the Battle of First Manassas. It was during a charge at Henry Hill that Charles was wounded in the hip. He resigned his commission as major, only to return to duty two more times.

After returning from the war, Charles viewed the destruction surrounding Roswell, and he decided to move his family to the crossroads of Chamblee-Dunwoody and Spalding Drive. Today, this location is the City of Dunwoody. Charles rebuilt the covered bridge over the Chattahoochee river in 1869; he charged a toll fee of twenty-five cents for a wagon and five cents for a person to cross. Charles opened the first post office in Dunwoody; he died in 1905 and was buried in Roswell's Presbyterian Church Cemetery. Ellen died in 1895 and was buried at Oakland Cemetery in Atlanta.

Dunwody Scottish Roots

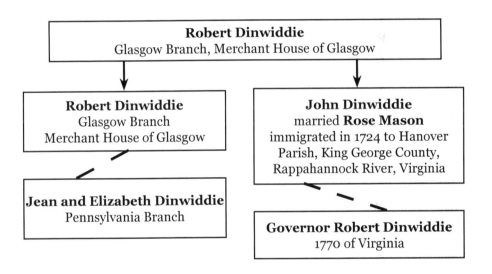

Alleyn Dinwithie (1290's)
Thomas Dinwiddie, Chief of Clan killed in 1503
Laird of Dunwoodie, killed in 1512
Dunwodie Castle, Dinwoodie Holm, Dinwoodie Green

Robert Dinwiddie
Glasgow Branch, Merchant House of Glasgow

Robert Dinwiddie
Glasgow Branch
Merchant House of Glasgow

John Dinwiddie
married **Rose Mason**
immigrated in 1724 to Hanover
Parish, King George County,
Rappahannock River, Virginia

Jean and Elizabeth Dinwiddie
Pennsylvania Branch

Governor Robert Dinwiddie
1770 of Virginia

71

Scotland - Ulster, Ireland - America
(another Pennsylvania Branch)

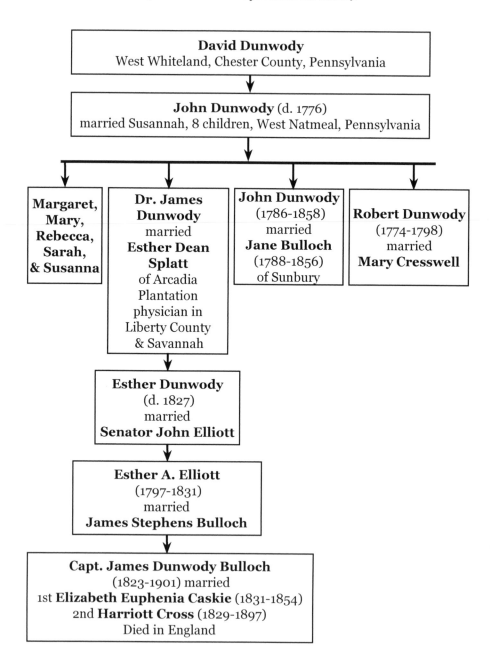

David Dunwody
West Whiteland, Chester County, Pennsylvania

John Dunwody (d. 1776)
married Susannah, 8 children, West Natmeal, Pennsylvania

Margaret, Mary, Rebecca, Sarah, & Susanna

Dr. James Dunwody
married
Esther Dean Splatt
of Arcadia Plantation physician in Liberty County & Savannah

John Dunwody (1786-1858)
married
Jane Bulloch (1788-1856)
of Sunbury

Robert Dunwody (1774-1798)
married
Mary Cresswell

Esther Dunwody (d. 1827)
married
Senator John Elliott

Esther A. Elliott (1797-1831)
married
James Stephens Bulloch

Capt. James Dunwody Bulloch (1823-1901) married
1st **Elizabeth Euphenia Caskie** (1831-1854)
2nd **Harriott Cross** (1829-1897)
Died in England

John and Jane Dunwody Family

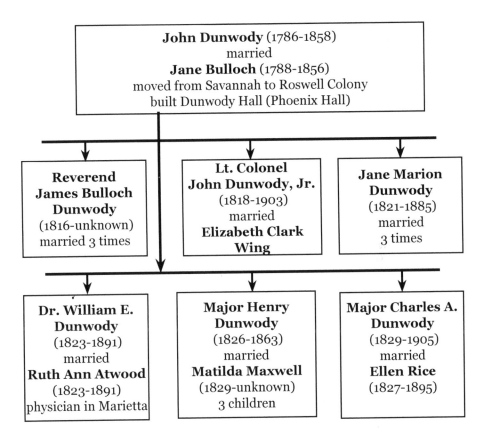

John Dunwody (1786-1858)
married
Jane Bulloch (1788-1856)
moved from Savannah to Roswell Colony
built Dunwody Hall (Phoenix Hall)

Reverend
James Bulloch
Dunwody
(1816-unknown)
married 3 times

Lt. Colonel
John Dunwody, Jr.
(1818-1903)
married
Elizabeth Clark
Wing

Jane Marion
Dunwody
(1821-1885)
married
3 times

Dr. William E.
Dunwody
(1823-1891)
married
Ruth Ann Atwood
(1823-1891)
physician in Marietta

Major Henry
Dunwody
(1826-1863)
married
Matilda Maxwell
(1829-unknown)
3 children

Major Charles A.
Dunwody
(1829-1905)
married
Ellen Rice
(1827-1895)

H. Smiths Arrive With General Oglethorpe

The name of Smith was first found in northern England and Scotland, where the family seat had been located since ancient times. These people were the Picts and forefathers of the Smiths. Smith is the most common name in Scotland.

John Smith Migrates to the Carolinas

The earliest ancestor of the Archibald Smith family was Reverend Archibald Smith of Scotland. His son, John Smith, married Eliza Williamson of Wales. They migrated to the new world with his friend, General James E. Oglethorpe, on his second visit to Georgia in 1749.

John and Eliza first settled in South Carolina; he operated a store in Beaufort, South Carolina. They eventually relocated to coastal Georgia. John became a wealthy plantation owner growing rice and cotton with the help of slave labor. As a reputable merchant from Charleston, he traveled with John McQueen and Jonathan Bryan in 1774. They were unsuccessful in completing their mission to negotiate a trade agreement with the Creek and Seminole Indians of Florida. He was buried on Savannah's Oatlands Island.

Archibald Smith (Sr.) Wealthy Businessman

Archibald Smith (Sr.), John's son, was very wealthy. He owned a wharf along the Savannah River and ran a ferry across the river. The Governor of South Carolina granted Archibald three islands in the Beaufort District near Fort Jackson, Georgia. They were Rabbit Island, Hog Island, and Long Island totaling 162 acres.

Archibald's first wife, Margaret Joyner Smith, died soon after delivering a stillborn daughter in 1794; she was buried in the St. Helene Church Yard, South Carolina. John Joyner Smith, their one surviving child, married into the Barnwell family. Archibald's second wife, Helen Zubly, of St. Marys, brought Blue Mud Plantation to the marriage. Her father was Reverend Hans Joachim Zubly of Swiss heritage. Archibald and Helen had two children who survived into adulthood, Eliza Z. Smith (1809-1846) and Archibald Smith (Jr.) (1801-1886) a founding father of Roswell.

When Archibald (Sr.) died in 1830, he was buried in Savannah's Colonial Cemetery. His holdings of the wharf, store, and three islands were willed to his descendants.

Archibald Smith (Jr.) Founder of Roswell

Archibald Smith's (Jr.) early years were spent in Savannah; he moved to St. Marys about the time of his father's demise in 1830. Archibald (Jr.) married Anne Magill, born in St. Marys in 1809. It was a marriage of convenience arranged by Eliza Smith, his sister, and lasted fifty years. Both Anne and Archibald's mothers were sisters from the Swiss Zubly family of Savannah.

The Seagroves were of German-Swiss descent and connected to the Zubly family. A Seagrove ancestor settled on a Bahama Island plantation. The Seagrove daughters were sent to Savannah for an education; they married and stayed in Georgia. Their descendants married into the Smith family of Roswell. Hence the name Seagrove and Zubly are found in the names chosen within the Smith generations.

The Smith home in St. Marys was the Appenzelle Plantation of Camden County. It was named after the Swiss canton from which Smith's wife's Zubly family emigrated. Smith also owned Jersey Point, north of St. Marys on Kings Bay. He tried to raise cotton on the Jersey Point Plantation and rice on Appenzelle Plantation but failed at both. (Today, a large United States Navy nuclear submarine support base is located in the center of Smith's Jersey Point Plantation).

Roswell King invited Archibald Smith (Jr.) to invest in his vision of a textile mill in north Georgia. Roswell and Archibald previously knew each other from early business interactions on the coast. Therefore, in December 1838, Archibald led his family into the wilds of north Georgia. He brought his wife, daughter Elizabeth Anne, son William Seagrove Smith, and two of Mrs. Smith's sisters, Helen Zubly Magill and Elizabeth Pye Magill. He also brought his slaves to work in the house and the fields. Smith wanted to build a Presbyterian community based upon agriculture.

By 1839, the Presbyterian Church and the Roswell Manufacturing Company were established in Roswell, Georgia. The other families built beautiful mansions, but the Smiths, being the last to build a permanent home, wanted a simple farmhouse. One mile north of the village's center, they purchased 4 ½ lots of land and initially cleared 9 acres. His Oakwood Farm consisted of forty acres of cotton, while his Roswell plantation grew potatoes, grains, and other vegetables. Smith owned almost five hundred acres of land. He enjoyed experimenting with various seeds and grasses; he was the first person to introduce Bermuda grass to this area. He farmed and lived on Oakwood Farm in Lebanon, Georgia, near present day North Fulton Regional Hospital. The Smith's permanent Roswell house was completed in 1844, and Smith continued to farm both sites. He kept notes on his many interests and plantings in a journal, which resides at the Georgia State Archives.

Smith found that the RMC mill dividends kept his family in food, shelter, and clothing during the Civil War. It was his only source of income. Smith was elected as secretary of the Roswell Manufacturing Company's Stockholder's Board.

As the Union troops entered Georgia, the remaining Smith family fled to Valdosta, Georgia. After the war, the Smiths returned to Roswell; they found little damage done to the actual house and started their lives over again.

As a religious man, Archibald was a charter member of the Presbyterian Church. Archibald and Anne raised four children, two sons served in the Confederacy. Archibald Smith died in 1886 and was buried in the Presbyterian Church Cemetery. His wife Anne, died one year later and was buried beside him.

Archibald and Anne Smith's Children
William S. Smith...Confederate Soldier

William S. Smith, *Willie,* (1834-1865) enlisted in the Savannah Volunteer Guards and was stationed at Fort Screven on Tybee Island for basic training. He was assigned to the Signal Corps on Little Ogeechee and Vernon Rivers. He was on duty in Savannah until the fall of the city in late 1864. Willie was among General Hardee's retreating forces through the Carolinas.

By 1865, Willie developed typhoid fever, erysipelas, and dysentery while he was attached to Hardee's staff. He was hospitalized in the Confederate Peace Hospital in Raleigh, North Carolina, and began to recover. After the Battle of Bentonville, Peace Hospital was closed, and Mrs. Mason, who had been nursing Willie, took him to her home and continued to nurse him. Willie died in July and was buried in Oakwood Cemetery, Raleigh, in the Mason's family plot.

Sisters Eliza and Helen

The Smith sisters, Eliza *Lizzie* and Helen Z., never married but stayed with their parents and kept house. Helen died in 1896 and Eliza in 1915. Both sisters were buried in the Presbyterian Church Cemetery; their graves were left unmarked.

Archibald *Archie* Smith

Archibald Smith, *Archie or Sonny,* (1844-1923) was born in Roswell, Georgia. He was the only Smith who married and produced Smith children. He enrolled at Georgia Military Institute (GMI) in Marietta in April 1862; as a cadet he was exempt from military service by Governor Brown's law of May 1863. With Sherman's Army on its *March to the Sea*, Archie was assigned to guard Savannah. His detachment was among the last to retreat from Savannah in 1864. Willie and Archie met in Hardeeville and said their goodbyes on Dec 22nd. Archie was the only Smith to visit Willie's grave after the war in 1869.

Archie married Gulielma Riley (1846-1921) in 1870 and sired three children. Back in Roswell, he owned a store selling spokes and hubs. In order to make a living, Archie moved to LaGrange, Georgia, with his family and Grandmother Riley after the death of his parents. In LaGrange, Archie tried farming, but was unsuccessful, and lived off of land leases, land sales, timber, and turpentine from his Georgia and Arkansas properties. They had three children while living in LaGrange.

Archie's Children
(Dr.) Archibald Smith
The Smith's son (Dr.) Archibald Smith (1874-1947) graduated from the University of Georgia in 1895 and University of Pennsylvania with a medical degree in 1899. He never married but was a prominent physician in Atlanta until his death.

Another child, **Frances Maner Smith** (1875-1939) attended Lewisburg Female Academy in West Virginia. She never married but kept house for her brother, Arthur.

Arthur William Smith...Last Of The Line
The last of Archibald Smith's line was Arthur William Smith (1881-1960) who married Mary Norvell at the age of sixty. Arthur was the grandson of Archibald Smith (Jr.). Arthur attended the Citadel in Charleston, South Carolina from 1898-99, graduated from the University of Georgia in 1902, and studied architecture in Paris from 1907-1909.

Returning to Atlanta, he worked as a chief designer for several firms. He was given credit for designing the Atlanta City Hall, a new educational building for the Roswell Presbyterian Church, and the old Roswell City Hall on Founders Square.

Smith Family

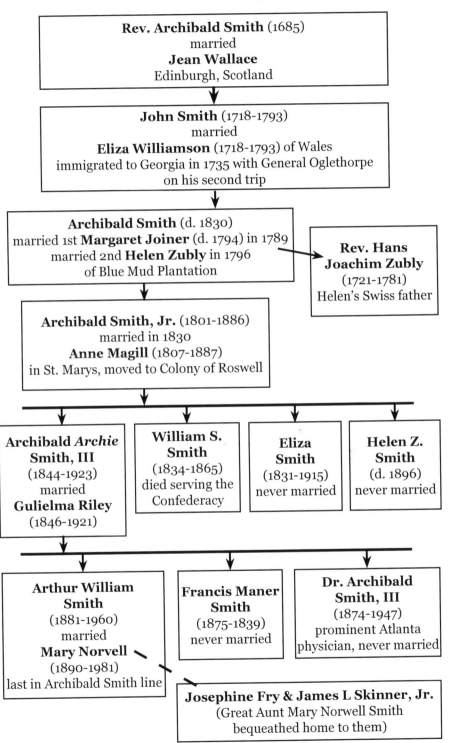

Rev. Archibald Smith (1685)
married
Jean Wallace
Edinburgh, Scotland

John Smith (1718-1793)
married
Eliza Williamson (1718-1793) of Wales
immigrated to Georgia in 1735 with General Oglethorpe
on his second trip

Archibald Smith (d. 1830)
married 1st **Margaret Joiner** (d. 1794) in 1789
married 2nd **Helen Zubly** in 1796
of Blue Mud Plantation

Rev. Hans Joachim Zubly
(1721-1781)
Helen's Swiss father

Archibald Smith, Jr. (1801-1886)
married in 1830
Anne Magill (1807-1887)
in St. Marys, moved to Colony of Roswell

Archibald *Archie* Smith, III
(1844-1923)
married
Gulielma Riley
(1846-1921)

William S. Smith
(1834-1865)
died serving the Confederacy

Eliza Smith
(1831-1915)
never married

Helen Z. Smith
(d. 1896)
never married

Arthur William Smith
(1881-1960)
married
Mary Norvell
(1890-1981)
last in Archibald Smith line

Francis Maner Smith
(1875-1839)
never married

Dr. Archibald Smith, III
(1874-1947)
prominent Atlanta physician, never married

Josephine Fry & James L Skinner, Jr.
(Great Aunt Mary Norwell Smith
bequeathed home to them)

Arthur realized that the Smith house had been closed for some time after Elizabeth's death (*Lizzie*) in 1915. Arthur decided to reopen the home in 1940 and live there during the summer months with his wife, Mary Norvell.

After Arthur's death in 1960, Mary remained in the Smith house with an African-American woman, Mamie Cotton, who took care of her. The Archibald Smith lineage ends with Arthur's death.

Mary Norvell Smith was a retired elementary school teacher from Atlanta, member of the DAR and Colonial Dames, and a trustee of the Rabun-Gap Nacoochee School. While traveling throughout Europe, she refurnished much of the Smith home. She was buried in Westview Cemetery in Atlanta. Being childless, Mary Norvell Smith willed the remaining Smith property to her niece, Josephine Fry Skinner in 1981. Josephine and her husband, James Lister Skinner Jr., preserved the house by transferring ownership to the City of Roswell.

I. Pratt English Lineage

The English name of Pratt has been common since the Middle Ages. Both Edmund and Charles Pratt were considered aristocracy during King Henry VIII's reign. There were Pratts who owned large tracts of land in Ireland as well.

Andrew Pratt of Hertfordshire, England, was the first documented ancestor of the Nathaniel A. Pratt line. His son, William Pratt remained in England, attended Cambridge, and became a minister of the Anglican Church at Stevenage, England. He did not come to America as some family records surmise, and he died in Stevenage. William married Elizabeth Prime and sired six children. Their two oldest sons, John and (Lt.) William were born in Stevenage, England.

John and William Pratt Arrive In The British Provinces

John and William Pratt migrated in 1630 from Plymouth, England, to America's British Colony. They were followers of Reverend Thomas Hooker and went to Newtown, Massachusetts. They traveled with other Puritans to Hartford, Connecticut, as original settlers in 1636, and moved after five years to Saybrook near the Connecticut River. Saybrook, later called Essex, was noted in genealogical records as Old Saybrook, a historical New England town. Fort Saybrook was one of Connecticut's oldest settlements and its first military fortification.

The younger brother, William Pratt (1609) migrated to Connecticut and fought in the Pequot Indian Wars with the rank of lieutenant. Lt. William married Elizabeth Clark also of Connecticut and sired eight children. Her father was a close friend of William, and they fought together in the Indian wars.

Old Saybrook Pratts

Jabez (or Jared, born 1710) married Abigail Clark also of Old Saybrook. They became grandparents of Nathaniel Alpheus Pratt, a founding father of Roswell, who obviously came from a long line of patriotic military families. Ezra Pratt son of Jabez and Abigail, married Temperance Southworth. Abigail's bloodline extended back to Captain William Southworth in 1659 from Plymouth, Massachusetts. (Southworth was an old Colonial family whose descendants filled the New England history books). They had eleven children and lived in Old Saybrook. One of Ezra Pratt's son was Nathaniel Alpheus, born in Old Saybrook, Connecticut.

Nathaniel A. Pratt Minister of Roswell

Nathaniel graduated from Yale College in 1820, and studied Theology at Princeton Theological Seminary. In 1823, he became ordained and licensed to preach by the New Brunswich Presbytery located in Shrewsbury, New Jersey. While at Princeton Theological Seminary, Pratt met Catherine Barrington King as she attended a northern finishing school. He became pastor of the Presbyterian Church of Darien leaving Old Saybrook in 1825. During his career, he assisted his older brother, Horace, in organizing the first Presbyterian Church in Tallahassee, Florida in 1832.

While Nathaniel Pratt was living in Darien, he inherited George and Charles Pratt, who were slaves belonging to James Hudson. When Hudson died in 1836, the slaves became Pratt's property and came with Pratt to Roswell. Charles Pratt, a slave, became a missionary to Africa with John Hale from Roswell. George Pratt, a slave, became an expert cabinetmaker in Atlanta; Pratt Street in Atlanta was named for him. Reverend Pratt believed in teaching his slaves to read and write although this practice was against Georgia law.

Nathaniel married Catherine Barrington King in March 1830 in Darien. Pratt was invited to organize Roswell's Presbyterian Church and become its first pastor. He held this position for forty years. Nathaniel moved his family to Roswell arriving on May 15, 1840, with his ten slaves. Their new home was completed in 1842; it was later called Great Oaks. The Pratts had eleven children. While in Roswell, Nathaniel traveled by horseback preaching to the mountain folk and a few Cherokees who were able to avoid the Indian evacuation.

Reverend Pratt died from a stroke in 1879, but Catherine lived many more years in post-war Roswell. Both were buried in Roswell's Presbyterian Church Cemetery.

Pratt Children

The Pratt children were highly educated and, while some became more famous than others, they all had the patriotic fervor for the Confederacy.

Horace A. Pratt

Horace A. Pratt, first son of the Pratts, was born in Darien, Horace married Lilias Logan from Virginia; they raised four children. He died in November 1870, near Charleston, South Carolina. She died one month after Horace in December 1870.

(Rev.) Henry Barrington Pratt

(Reverend) Henry Barrington Pratt joined the Confederate Army as a chaplain. Born in Darien, Georgia, he attended Oglethorpe University and was ordained by the Cherokee Presbytery in 1855. He married Joanna Frances Gildersleeve, and served ten years as a missionary in Bogota, Columbia, after the American Civil War.

He translated the American Bible into the Spanish language in 1893; this brought Henry a great deal of fame among the Hispanic Protestants. Encouraged, he opened a Bible training school in Texas for Mexicans and Christian workers. After the school closed in 1899, Henry served as pastor to a Hispanic congregation in Brooklyn, New York. He died in 1912 and was buried in Hackensack, New Jersey.

(Dr.) Nathaniel A. Pratt Jr.

(Dr.) Nathaniel A. Pratt Jr., was born in Darien and matriculated at Oglethorpe College majoring in chemistry and geology. After graduating from Savannah's Medical College in 1856, he continued his scientific studies at the Lawrence Scientific School located at Harvard University, Boston.

83

Dr. Pratt was a scientist and decided never to practice medicine, but to devote his life to chemistry, mineralogy, and geology. In 1855, he married Julia Stubbs from Milledgeville and sired seven children. He was professor of chemistry at the Savannah Medical College and later at Oglethorpe University, until the war broke out in 1861. He created the Confederate company, Jordan Grays, in May 1861. His destiny was not on the battlefield, but as Assistant Chief of the Confederate State's Niter and Mining Bureau with the rank of captain.

After the war, Dr. Pratt was involved in various mining endeavors and manufacturing of commercial fertilizers. He became professor of applied science at Washington and Lee University from 1872-1876. Returning to Georgia, he was a chemist for the state and lived in Decatur, Georgia. In 1906, he was killed by a train on the Georgia railroad and buried in Decatur Cemetery.

Charles Jones Pratt

Charles Jones Pratt, born in Darien, became a Civil engineer after attending the Marietta's Georgia Military Institute (GMI). He enlisted in May 1862, in the Savannah Volunteer Guards, Co. A 18th Battalion Georgia Infantry and was appointed drillmaster at Macon's instruction camp. Early in 1863, Charles enlisted as 1st Lt. Co. B Roswell Battalion Georgia Cavalry. By 1864, he joined Morgan's Command Co. B 11th regiment Kentucky Cavalry and was taken prisoner in Green County, Tennessee, in September 1864. Fortunately, he was exchanged two weeks later at Rough and Ready, Georgia.

In 1867, Charles married Emma Stubbs, sister of Julia, who was married to his brother Nathaniel, and sired six children. His career included various jobs such as assistant city engineer in Atlanta, engineer for Louisville and Nashville Railroad, and engineer for the construction of the Florida East Coast Railroad from Miami to Key West. Charles died in Atlanta in 1924 and was buried in Decatur Cemetery.

Katherine Quintard Pratt

Katherine Quintard Pratt (Heath) was born in Roswell and married Alfred T. Heath, a farmer from Florida. They bore four children. Her father's Academy school was left in her care after his death. She taught at the Academy for many years. She died at the age of 89 and was buried in West View Cemetery Atlanta, Georgia.

Other Pratt Children

Bayard Hand Pratt, born in Darien, married Mattie Wood from Alabama and sired six children. Francis Lorinda Pratt married John Baker; she died at the age of twenty-two. They had a daughter named for her mother, but the child died as an infant. He remarried and had five children. In 1880, Isabella Julia Pratt married Reverend Walker, a teacher from Ohio. Sarah Anna Pratt was born in Darien; she was seventeen years old when the Civil War began. William Nephew Pratt, born in Darien, married Elvira Maloney. They raised four children, and in 1880, William became a farmer in Acworth, Georgia.

Pratt English Roots

Pratt name
(Seals of Suffolk, Berkshire, and Essex)
during the 12th and 13th centuries

Edmund Pratt	**Charles Pratt**
Lord of the Manor	Earl of Camden,
	Lord Chief Justice of England

Joshua Pratt	**Andrew Pratt**
immigrated to America in 1623	married **Ellen Marsh**
Constable at Plymouth	Hertfordshire, England

Rev. William Pratt (1562-1629)
married **Elizabeth Prime**
pastor at Stevenage, England

Old Saybrook Pratts begin here

Lt. William Pratt (1609-1678)
married **Elizabeth Clark** (1620-1665)
born in Stevenage, England

Capt. William Pratt (1653-1717)
married **Hannah Kirkland** (1662-1719)

Benjamin Pratt (1680-unknown)
married **Ann Bates** (1678-unknown)

Jabez (Jared) Pratt (1710-1764)
married **Abigail Clark** (1720-1784)

Ezra Pratt (1757-1806)
married **Temperance Southworth**
(1759-1842)

Rev. Nathaniel Alpheus Pratt (1796-1806)
married **Catherine Barrington King** (1810-1895)

Nathaniel Alpheus Pratt Family

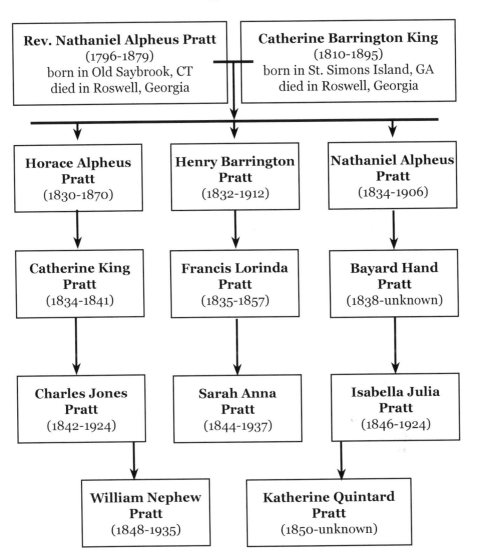

Rev. Nathaniel Alpheus Pratt
(1796-1879)
born in Old Saybrook, CT
died in Roswell, Georgia

Catherine Barrington King
(1810-1895)
born in St. Simons Island, GA
died in Roswell, Georgia

Horace Alpheus Pratt
(1830-1870)

Henry Barrington Pratt
(1832-1912)

Nathaniel Alpheus Pratt
(1834-1906)

Catherine King Pratt
(1834-1841)

Francis Lorinda Pratt
(1835-1857)

Bayard Hand Pratt
(1838-unknown)

Charles Jones Pratt
(1842-1924)

Sarah Anna Pratt
(1844-1937)

Isabella Julia Pratt
(1846-1924)

William Nephew Pratt
(1848-1935)

Katherine Quintard Pratt
(1850-unknown)

Part 3 Historic Buildings of Roswell

Many of Roswell's historic buildings and mansions were built between 1839-1848; they are not replicas but have undergone some degree of restoration through the years. Few Southern towns have such pristine early 19th century houses. The Roswell houses are of several different architectural designs including Greek Revival, Raised Cottage, Georgian Colonial, or Vernacular.

Roswell Presbyterian Church

The Historic Roswell Presbyterian Church remains the oldest public building in the city, and the first church incorporated in Cobb County. Roswell King donated land for the church to ensure it would be the center of town. The town limits extended one mile from the church in every direction. The Greek Revival design, suggested by Willis Ball, was much to the liking of Roswell residents. Roswell King closely supervised the construction of the church in 1840. He had gained extensive building expertise executing his Darien projects.

The interior of the church is reminiscent of a New England meeting house with boxed pews, plastered walls, blown glass windows, raised pulpit, and a balcony or gallery designated for the slaves, who were also members. Some pews have nameplates of families who sat there each Sunday. The church is topped with a small square bell tower instead of a spire. The bell was cast in

1826 in Philadelphia; it was given as a gift to the church from the Independent Church of Savannah. The exterior façade of the church contains a Doric-columned portico, symmetrical windows on each side of the door, and a pediment gable. The Reverend Nathaniel A. Pratt was its first pastor and continued to minister there for the next thirty-nine years.

Reverend Pratt became concerned for the safety of his church when he learned of approaching Federal troops following the Battle of Kennesaw Mountain in 1864. He gave the sanctuary Bible to a family who fled south and the silver communion service set to the mill superintendent, Olney Eldridge.

Mr. Eldridge sought out Fanny Whitmire who was a reliable church member and mill worker. He asked her to hide the communion set somewhere in her modest mill house. Fanny ran home to hide the set. Her mother suggested hiding it inside a basket of quilting scraps. Fanny was one of the mill workers who charged with treason in the coming weeks by General Garrard. The soldiers never found the service set. Her mother later returned the set safely to the church.

The sanctuary Bible remained missing until one hundred years later when the Bible was returned by a family in Louisiana. Both items are now safely on display in the church's history room. The church's organ was removed from the sanctuary, and it was destroyed by the weather when left outside during the Union occupation.

The Academy

Education was as important to these families as their religion. They built a log house north of the church site to provide for the education of the children of both sexes. The primitive structure was soon replaced with a two-room brick Greek Revival building. The first schoolhouse was called the Academy and

Historic Presbyterian Church, author's photograph

completed in 1840. The Academy's first teacher was Rev. Aaron Hicks Hand, a Presbyterian minister from Augusta and youngest brother of Bayard E. Hand, Elizabeth King Hand's husband.

Upon graduation from the Academy, young men had the opportunity to attend Reverend Pratt's preparatory school prior to college. Pratt's preparatory school was located behind the Pratt's house in a comfortable, small study near the barn.

Many buildings replaced the Academy, but their purpose remained to educate children. The church continued to administer the school until some time in the 1870's, when the school was deeded to the town of Roswell. The Academy became both a public elementary and high school in 1892.

By 1914, the public school was torn down and replaced with a new two-story building that included first through tenth grades. In 1925, Georgia code prohibited minors less than sixteen years of age, from working in mills and factories; therefore, the public school included the eleventh grade in the 1920's. Black children were segregated to a public school on Oxbo Road, which included one through seventh grades. Today, the Fulton County Teaching Museum resides on the old Academy and public school site.

Primrose Cottage

Roswell King had one person in mind when he ordered the construction of Primrose Cottage, his daughter Elizabeth King Hand. Primrose Cottage was hastily begun in January and completed in August, 1839. Elizabeth and her children moved into the home in early 1840 with Roswell King joining them.

Primrose has elements of Georgian Colonial architecture with five windows on the front façade, separated panes of glass, bookend chimneys, clapboard construction, a small overhang above a columned portico, and a veranda on the back facade. The interior features three stories with a large open hall, which connects two deep rooms on either side of the hall flowing into each other. A staircase is located in the rear of the hall.

Roswell King ordered an unusual feature built in front of the property; it was a white fence with individually turned balusters. Peter Minhinnett, a carpenter from England, built the rosemary-pine fence; Roswell King wanted each home to have this type of fencing, but it never happened.

Primrose Cottage hosted the organization of the church with fifteen members, while the church was under construction. Primrose was also a wonderful location for the newly arriving families to come together and discuss their future.

This was Roswell King's last residence; he died in Barrington King's home sitting in a rocking chair. One week prior to his death, Elizabeth Hand moved her family to Rome, Georgia, on February 7, 1844. She remarried two years later.

Primrose Cottage, author's photograph

Primrose had several different owners including the Kings, Camps, Wings, and Ruckers. Today, it is a privately-owned events facility.

Bulloch Hall

This grand Greek Revival mansion was built for Major James Stephens Bulloch and his wife Martha in late 1839. They resided for a time in an abandoned Cherokee house, waiting for their home to be built. The Cherokee house was located in today's Martin's Landing subdivision.

Willis Ball designed this clapboard mansion. The house's floor plan used the popular *4 square* common to this style. The main level included a wide central hall flanked by two large rooms on each side and two small rooms in the rear. In the back was a warming room and a nursery. The downstairs hall arch was supported with two Doric columns, and the fireplace mantels had hand-carved columns.

The second floor consisted of four bedrooms and a front sewing room. Cross ventilation of cool breezes were available by opening windows, which extend from the floor to the ceiling on the main floor. The windows, when fully open, allowed the residents and visitors easy access to the outside. A kitchen, wine cellar, cold storage room, and a casual dining area were located in the above ground basement level in the rear.

The exterior facade has twenty-one foot high columns that are one hundred and thirteen inches in circumference and are actually hollow inside. The house's driveway is heart-shaped. The grounds were landscaped under Major Bulloch's oversight. He planted thirty-seven varieties of ornamental shade and fruit trees. Today, many of the original trees survive, and Osage orange trees still protect the property from pesky insects.

The plantation was originally ten acres and majestically stands at the end of Bulloch Avenue. Slave quarters and carriage house replica structures are located near the house and enhance one's idea of life in the antebellum South.

In 1856, Martha was living in New York City with Mittie, so she rented the property to Thomas King and his wife. After Martha's death in 1864, Dr. West, her son-in-law, was finally able to sell the property to Jason Sylvester Wood in 1872. Jason Wood sold Bulloch Hall in 1888 to Eugene Wood. By 1892, Laurel Mills Manufacturing Company owned Bulloch Hall and later sold it to Isaac Robert in 1898 along with Primrose Cottage. In 1905, Jehu Bartow Wing rented the property and bought it two years later. Jehu's widow, Hattie Wing lived in Bulloch Hall until after WWII.

The house remained closed for the next twenty years, until it was sold in 1971 to Richard Myrick, who restored much of the

Bulloch Hall, author's photograph

house. The City of Roswell finally bought Bulloch Hall in 1978. Today, Bulloch Hall is a house museum designed enriching future generations with Roswell history.

Barrington Hall

Willis Ball designed Barrington Hall as a Greek Revival mansion for the president of a successful company. When the Barrington King family arrived in 1838, they lived in a log cabin called the *Castle*, which Roswell King had built. As more families migrated to Roswell, the Barrington King family moved into a small clapboard-framed house on their property, allowing others to reside in the *Castle*. That little framed house would soon be used as a kitchen, once the main house was completed in 1842. The timbers were cut from the King property and aged two years before the building of the mansion. An English landscape gardener designed the grounds.

Barrington Hall is a true example of Greek Revival architecture; it is the largest of the homes with eleven rooms and five thousand square feet. It has five bedrooms each with a private dressing room. The interior walls have horsehair plaster, heart pine floors, and walnut doors. Three of the four exterior facades have Doric columns, with fourteen columns in all. It is the only Roswell mansion claiming to be continuously lived in since its completion.

The Barrington Hall estate overlooked the mill valley, Vickery Creek, and the Chattahoochee River. Originally, the property claimed over forty acres with gardens, fruit trees, and arbors; the grounds contain much less acreage today. Barrington Hall estate was not considered a working plantation; Barrington was a businessman and not a planter. The property consisted of the house, smoke house, icehouse, kitchen, slave quarters, carriage house, barn, pasture, orchard, and vegetable garden.

During the Union occupation, the house was used as headquarters for the Federal officers with General Kenner Garrard residing there. After the troops left Roswell, itinerant families moved into the house, living in all of the rooms. When Colonel Barrington Simeral King came home to Barrington Hall with his wife and children in early 1865, he cleared the trespassers out of the house. His wife Bessie took charge of getting the house ready for Barrington and Catherine's return.

Meanwhile, Colonel King returned to his troops and was killed leading a charge at Aversboro, North Carolina, on March 10, 1865. His body was brought home in February 1866 and re-interred in the Presbyterian Church Cemetery.

When Barrington King died, his daughter Eva Baker and her family moved into Barrington Hall from Virginia to care for Catherine Margaret King, her mother. When Mrs. King died in 1887, the Bakers stayed and raised their children in Barrington Hall. Evelyn Baker died in 1923, and her grandchild, Evelyn Simpson eventually bought the property with her mother, Kate, from the other descendants.

Evelyn and her younger sister, Katherine Simpson lived in Barrington Hall. They never married; Evelyn died in 1960 leaving everything to Katherine. After living alone for fourteen more years, Katherine asked her closest friend, Lois Carson to move in with her. Eventually Katherine legally adopted Lois in 1977 so that Lois could inherit Barrington Hall. Lois legally changed her name to Lois King Simpson.

Barrington Hall, author's photograph

Katherine died in 1995 at 99 years of age. As time passed, Lois was unable to pay for the house's enormous maintenance costs, and the house fell into disrepair. In 1987, a fire started from faulty wiring, destroying the roof; the water and fire caused damage throughout the house. Because the house was not insured, donations from volunteers and local businesses rebuilt the roof and painted the house.

Lois Simpson died in 2003. Mrs. Sarah Winner and Mr. Hunter, her husband, acquired the property and restored much of the house. As a result of her efforts, Mrs. Winner won the 2003 Excellence in Restoration Award from the Georgia Trust for Historic Preservation.

Finally, the property was sold to the City of Roswell in 2005 and was opened to the public. Today Barrington Hall provides community educational programs emphasizing the lives of the King, Baker and Simpson families of Roswell. The home is furnished with many of the original possessions of those families.

Dunwody Hall

Willis Ball designed Dunwody Hall in 1842 for John and Jane Dunwody. The property consisted of twelve acres. The Dunwody family stayed at Charles Wolford's mill keeper's house while waiting for their Roswell home to be completed. The mill keeper's house was located in Lebanon, where the entrance to Roswell Apartments is located today.

Dunwody Hall's exterior is a mirror image of the Greek Revival Bulloch Hall. The mansion has large walk-in closets or dressing rooms and a second set of stairs from a back hallway to the landing of the front stairs. These stairs allowed the slaves a private way to go between the floors and not disturb the family.

On the night of its housewarming party, the home caught fire from a piece of lumber left wedged inside of the chimney. The family fled with their belongings and rebuilt the house by 1847. This time, instead of lumber, the exterior was faced with brick and covered in stucco to resemble stone. The Dunwodys renamed the house Phoenix Hall, since it rose from the ashes of their previous house.

The front facade of the house has four massive Doric columns, which supports a two-story portico. The original kitchen was located in the above ground basement. The home still has its original woodwork, sashes, shutters, and boxwood shrubbery.

General Andrew Jackson Hansell of Marietta acquired Dunwody Hall in 1869. At one time after the war, General Hansell was the president of Roswell Manufacturing Company. Mrs. Hansell renamed the house Mimosa Hall, because Mimosa trees lined the entry from the gate to the front door. These pink-flowered trees were brought from Darien, Georgia.

Dunwody Hall, author's photograph

In 1899, the property was sold to James King's widow, Meta Lewis. Once more it was sold, this time to Neel Reid in 1916. As an Atlanta architect, Reid redesigned the gardens and laid the stone courtyard in the shape of a champagne glass. (The original courtyard was heart shaped). By 1947, the property had reverted back to the Hansell descendants. Today, it is occupied by a descendant of General Hansell.

Great Oaks

Reverend Nathaniel A. Pratt and his wife Catherine King Pratt built Great Oaks (Pratt House) in 1842. The house is a good example of Georgian Colonial architecture. Originally, the design chosen was Greek Revival like the other mansions in Roswell. Fate had different plans; the seasoned timber for framing the house caught fire and was destroyed. The Pratts did not want to wait two more years for more timber to be aged. Instead, the Reverend instructed his slaves to make bricks by hand and lay them in a Flemish bond pattern; this alone changed the house design. The other features of the exterior took on elements of Georgian Colonial, possibly suggested by Willis Ball.

The house has three stories with eighteen-inch thick masonry walls. Heart pine flooring was placed throughout and enhanced the carved mantels and woodwork. Several features make this house quite unique. It has a good morning staircase at the upstairs central landing, where the bedrooms are located. A three-room dormitory was located on the third floor, probably designed for the many Pratt children to enjoy.

The main floor consists of two front parlors, a study, dining room, and winter kitchen located in the rear. This home also had a summer kitchen and outbuildings connected by a lovely covered walkway. Today, there are two attached verandas at which are not original to the home. The property was heavily farmed with corn, wheat, and sorghum. Beautiful oak trees were plentiful around the house.

The Pratts remained in their home when the Union troops arrived in 1864. General Garrard's Union Cavalry were housed among the fields and grounds. It was reported that General Jonathan "Black Jack" Logan and other officers shared the house with the Pratts, who resided on the third floor. Many of Reverend Platt's letters written to absent Roswell families still exist; they described the activities in Roswell while under Union occupation. The Pratts survived the war and remained in Roswell.

Four generations of Pratts owned Great Oaks until 1981. Education was important to the minister who had attended both Yale and Princeton. He recognized his daughter's zeal to continue to support education and the history of the home; as a result the house was passed down to Katherine Quintard Pratt Heath. She

Great Oaks, author's photograph

married Alfred Taylor Heath; their family moved to Atlanta in 1887 and rented the Pratt home to local families.

In 1921, Mrs. Heath's son-in-law, Arthur Jesse Merrill bought the house and property for his wife, Natalie Heath Merrill. Great Oaks became her summer home. They replaced the original columned porch with a stoop and altered the front façade. The Merrills named Pratt's house, Great Oaks, as we know it today.

A fire destroyed Pratt's study and many of the oak trees on the southern side of the property in 1931. A fishpond, garden, and tennis court once resided near the house but have long disappeared. After Mrs. Merrill's demise in 1938, her daughter Natalie Heath Merrill Rushin and son Arthur Jessie Merrill Jr. inherited Great Oaks. The home once again became rental property with absent landlords.

Finally in 1945, the Rushin family bought out the Merrills and moved into the home to raise their sons. By 1981, Great Oaks was sold to Edward and Colleen Briesemeister who installed air conditioning, a new heating system, and new wiring. The property was sold in 2002 to James Hugh and Linda Lively. Today, it is a private-event facility, and the house and landscaping are kept in pristine condition.

Smith Plantation

The Smith property is truly the only plantation in the early Colony of Roswell; it was the home of Archibald and Ann Magill Smith. The plantation is situated about one mile north of the Presbyterian Church near present day Norcross Street. The house is quite different from the other stately mansions of the original founders. Mr. and Mrs. Smith's farmhouse is a design called vernacular architecture. It suited their lifestyle and was constructed of hand-planed timber from trees grown on the plantation. A separate kitchen, servant houses, carriage house,

Smith Plantation, author's photograph

and barn were made of this worked timber. A caretaker's cottage and corncrib are also present on the property, ten buildings in all. (The second floor porch roof and supporting columns are not original to the house but added sometime during the 20th century).

The Smith house eventually became property of the City of Roswell. Today, the home contains all of the original furniture of the Smith family descendants. The house and surrounding grounds are open to the public as a museum, testifying to the lifestyle of an antebellum farmer.

Holly Hill

Holly Hill is located on Mimosa Avenue facing the square; it was the last of the homes built in 1847 and sat on two acres of ground. This home was designed as a raised cottage summer retreat for Robert Adams Lewis and family. Robert was a Savannah cotton broker who also had served as mayor and Inferior Court Justice of Savannah. His wife, Catherine Barrington Cooke was a niece of Catherine Barrington King and her namesake. When the Lewis family decided to make Roswell their permanent home, they brought their slaves and furnishings from Savannah.

The house has broad steps leading to a main floor, which contains a kitchen, dining hall, and food larders. The front facade has a Doric-columned piazza with a duplicate on the back of the house. The interior is typical of this style with a central hall separating double parlors and two bedrooms. Mantels are made of Black Italian marble and were transported from Savannah to adorn the parlors. The second floor has additional bedroom space.

The Lewis family sold the property and moved in 1855, eight years after the home was built. Their daughter, Elizabeth Catherine Lewis, married Roswell King's grandson, James Audley Maxwell King, in 1860, at Robert Lewis' new home on Staten Island, New York.

Robert Lewis died in January 1906 and was buried at Dorchester Cemetery in Liberty County, Georgia. The Lewis family is not considered to be one of the founders but the home remains as a testament to the Southern way of life prior to the war. James R. King, Barrington's son, bought Holly Hill and lived there after the war.

Holly Hill, author's photograph

I WANT TO KNOW MORE ABOUT:

ARCHITECTURE IN ROSWELL
GREEK REVIVAL ARCHITECTURE

Archaeological expeditions of Greece in the late 18th and early 19th centuries fueled the desire to emulate its ancient columned temples. This form of architecture was known as Greek Revival. Early 19th century American Southerners believed that ancient Greece represented a spirit of independence and democracy similar to their own. They wanted their homes to reflect this classical style, and brought European-trained architects to design Southern mansions in this popular Grecian style.

This style consists of classic clapboard exteriors with bold but simple lines. Entry porches are supported with

Doric columns. Decorative pilasters are often used both on the interior and exterior facades. A pilaster is a rectangular support that resembles a flat column. The front door is centered with a symmetrical number of windows. Near the roof is a pediment, a triangular gable that is located above the door. This style often incorporates a frieze or a horizontal band across doorways, windows or below the cornice.

RAISED COTTAGE ARCHITECTURE

Raised cottage architecture is found in the South's low country. These houses are elevated on a raised foundation basement and have a welcoming porch to enjoy warm breezes. Generally the roof is gabled with contoured bookend chimneys. The design was influenced by the French and Creoles.

These homes are designed with certain aspects of tidewater regional homes that are found in hot humid climates. The windows are designed to capture coastal breezes and highlight coastal views. This style's purpose was to provide surroundings with an air of comfort and romance for those who lived there.

GEORGIAN COLONIAL ARCHITECTURE

Georgian Colonial is a stately and symmetrical architecture that imitates the elaborate English Georgian homes. It arrived in New England and the South during the 1700's. Some of its features are adaptations from the Italian Renaissance. These features are square and symmetrical with a paneled centered front door. There is a medium pitched roof with minimal overhang, and flattened columns on each side of the door. Often five windows are placed across the front having small separated windowpanes.

VERNACULAR ARCHITECTURE

Vernacular architecture is based on regional tradition and local materials. It evolved over time reflecting cultural, technological, and economic values based on the need of its owners.

Part 4 The Textile Mills of Roswell

During 1835 and 1836, Roswell King bought Fannin Brown's land lottery acreage. One year later, Roswell, Barrington, Ralph, and many slaves cleared the land for a road leading to the location of the first mill. They built a thirty-foot dam creating a waterfall and a wooden millrace to carry water to power the mill.

Roswell King hired Henry Merrell, textile engineer from Utica, New York, to operate the 1839 factory. Merrell supervised the mill machinery installation, and by 1841, the mill was fully operational with twenty-eight employees. Merrell remained the mill supervisor for three more years, until he left to start his own cotton mill in Clark County, Georgia.

The 1839 mill operated efficiently over the next several years; by 1850, one hundred and fifty employees worked for RMC. The factory was producing yarn, shirting material, and a heavy cloth for sacks and work clothes called osnaburg. There was a great demand for finished cotton products. When Roswell King died in 1844, his dream was fulfilled, but RMC had not yet reached its full potential.

Barrington and the RMC Board of Directors agreed to fund another cotton factory and an addition to the 1839 mill, which had reached capacity. The mill was turning out one thousand pounds of yarn per day, using five bales of cotton. The new two-story wing added eight frames or looms and 1152 more spindles. It was predicted the extension would make an additional 650 pounds of yarn and 400 more pounds of cotton rope.

By 1852, RMC had built a wool factory (in 1846), a gristmill, shoe shop, and two blacksmith shops. A larger cotton factory with four and one-half stories was operational in 1854 (mill #2); it was located hundreds of feet upstream above the 1839 original mill site. A two-story machine shop was also built near the creek and sat between the two cotton mills. The RMC work force had doubled by 1855. RMC bought and operated Lebanon mill and produced 300 pounds of flour each day. In 1859, RMC bought acreage from Aaron Butler, which had been originally Cherokee Land and part of the Georgia land lottery.

RMC was not the only mill operating on Vickery Creek in Roswell. Barrington's sons, James and Thomas King, were motivated to own and operate their own mill. They financed and built a woolen mill in 1857 at the end of Vickery Creek, which emptied into the Chattahoochee River. It was named Ivy Mill and had an office/manager's residence on the hill above the mill's dam named, Allenbrooke. Ivy Mills made a wool/cotton blend of cloth that earned the name Roswell Gray. During the war, the mill sold this cloth to the Confederacy for uniforms. The cloth was warmer than flannel and did not shrink like wool when wet.

The Roswell mills were critical to the Confederacy's supply of roping, sheeting, tenting, and cloth for uniforms. The ordered products were sent to the Confederate Quarter Master located in Atlanta. Militia uniforms were first made from Roswell's cloth, but as the demand for cloth dramatically increased, there was insufficient quantity and only officer's uniforms were made from Roswell Gray.

Conditions for Millworkers

The textile mill was a dangerous place to work, whether mills were located in New England or Georgia. The atmosphere was kept extremely hot and humid, so that the cotton thread would not dry out. The noise level of the clattering machinery was so high that the loom girls had to shout to the person standing beside her.

A huge leather belt powered by water was always moving and weighed about nine hundred pounds. The revolving cylinder pulled the huge rubber belt from the first floor to the top of the mill. Hanks of someone's hair could be drawn to the belt and yank the worker up to the ceiling. If a worker inadvertently had a hand caught in the belt, the worker could be pulled up to the ceiling and squashed.

The combing of the cotton was generally done on the lowest floor of the mill. The danger here was from the carding machine, which could amputate fingers.

The workers continuously inhaled cotton lint dust fibers. Over time these fibers caused severe lung problems such as brown lung disease, chronic bronchitis, bronchial asthma, and frequent upper respiratory infections. Workers who fed thread into the looms and sucked the thread through the eye of the shuttle were at an even higher risk of lung issues. This process was called the *kiss of death.*

The Southern mill workers were given the unusual nickname, *lint heads,* since the lint settled on their hair and clothing. This was not a respectable label. The mill company controlled the workers' lives. They dictated where the worker lived, what they ate, and what they wore. The workers were not paid if they were injured or ill and missed their shift. Alcohol was strictly forbidden; Roswell was known as a dry town until after 1890. Management wanted the millworkers to be sober for safety reasons, and not to lose a day of labor due to intoxication, hangover, or injury.

Millworkers labored long hours from dawn until dusk. By 1890, Georgia legislature began to regulate all cotton and wool manufacturers; a worker was not to exceed eleven hours per day or sixty-six hours per week.

Destruction!

Roswell was invaded by Union troops on July 5, 1864. General William T. Sherman, Commander, sent General Kenner Garrard to locate several crossings of the Chattahoochee River for the Union troops to use after the Battle of Kennesaw Mountain. As part of Sherman's total war strategy, all manufacturing mills were to be burned as the Union soldiers advanced and fought toward Atlanta from Chattanooga, Tennessee, through the north Georgia mountains. If a mill was found to be producing goods for the Confederacy, it was immediately destroyed.

Upon reaching Roswell, Garrard saw that the mills were fully operational by women, children, and men. As a result, Roswell King's mill complex was burned, fifteen buildings in all including Ivy Mill's woolen mill. Theodore Roche, an Ivy mill weaver, attempted unsuccessfully to prevent the mill's destruction by claiming neutrality under the French flag. After the war, a new mill was built near the old mill site.

Roswell Manufacturing Company continued to operate after the death of Barrington King in 1866. George Camp was elected president of RMC. When George Camp resigned, Andrew Jackson Hansell succeeded him in 1867 and moved to Roswell from Marietta.

RMC built Willeo Cotton mill in 1873 and a new mill on Vickery Creek in 1882, now called Mill #2. A large turbine was installed on the original 1839 factory site to update the factories' hydraulic system. In 1886, the 1854 mill received a new water wheel.

RMC experienced a financial decline in the 1880s and 1890s, and was sold between 1920-1923. The new owners called the factories, Roswell Mills. The 1854 mill (now mill #1), the picker house, and warehouse were destroyed by lightening in 1926; but the 1882 mill survived and expanded to double its size. During World War II, the 1882 mill specialized in carpet backing and laundry netting as it continued to produce cotton yarn and cloth.

In 1947, Southern Mills bought Roswell Mills. Mimms Enterprises purchased the 1882 mill from Southern Mills for small offices and shops. The 1882 mill continued to operate until 1975 as *The Mill.*

A New Era for Georgia

Georgia experienced an industrial rebirth between 1870 and 1890. Northern money and manufacturing capital provided for the rebuilding of Atlanta, extending the railroad network, and increasing the number of Georgia mills from forty to seventy. The International Cotton Exposition of 1881, held in Piedmont Park, made Georgia the leading Southern state of manufacturing goods. It was said that over two-thirds of Georgia was farmland by 1882, and cotton dominated the manufacturing scene.

I WANT TO KNOW MORE ABOUT:

GEORGIA COTTON MILLS

Alexander Hamilton anticipated the need for a New South in his writings of 1775. He concluded that cotton mills should be close to where cotton was grown. The colonies were on the brink of the industrial revolution; New England led the textile industry in the north. Textile mills were perfectly suited for water-powered plants. Georgia's fall line caused the formation of waterfalls along her commercial rivers; this gave Georgia a geographical advantage in the pioneering of water-powered mills. With the invention of the cotton gin, seedless raw cotton was now easier to manufacture. Georgia also had abundant slave labor to harvest cotton. These three conditions resulted in Georgia becoming the leader in manufacturing of raw cotton.

The Georgia fall line is twenty miles wide running northeast from Columbus to Augusta, Georgia. It had a significant impact on colonial transportation and commerce. The fall line contains shoals and waterfalls that impede navigation but encouraged the building of dams to harness the power of the rivers. Chattahoochee, Ocmulgee, Oconee and Savannah Rivers were the main means of transportation with Macon, Milledgeville and Augusta as early centers of transportation and trade.

Jacob Gregg was the pioneer cotton manufacturer in Georgia. He built his own machinery at Whatley's gristmill between Madison and Monticello, Georgia, making yarn until 1816. Near Washington, Georgia, the second cotton mill was established where Eli Whitney first operated his invention. It had 160 spindles and was quite successful, but later abandoned in 1816 because of post-War of 1812 competition.

For the next twenty years, economic upheaval caused planters and farmers to migrate to rich cotton lands in Alabama, Missouri, Louisiana, Arkansas, and Texas. Georgia needed to keep its industrial wealth; the state government encouraged the growth of cotton manufacturing mills. By 1834, the Chattahoochee River's water power was being harnessed at Columbus, Georgia, to operate cotton mills.

Augusta had a factory to make its own spindle frames in its machine shop.

Then in 1839, Roswell King built his spinning and weaving factory in Roswell, while Athens, Georgia, boasted of three cotton factories. The Georgia census of 1840 lists 19 cotton mills employing 779 employees. By 1847, there were 28 cotton factories in 15 counties of Georgia. One year later, there were 32 cotton mills in Georgia with an investment of $2,000,000 and supported 6,000 workers and their families. These mills used 20,000 bales of cotton to make yarn and cloth. One third of all goods produced by these mills were being sold outside of Georgia. Georgia became known as the New England of the South, testing the economic giant, Massachusetts.

The industrial revolution increased Georgia's population, the building of railroads, and the number of factories. The economy of Georgia greatly improved because of the expansion and diversification that industry reflected. No longer would the South depend totally on the whims of raw cotton and rice prices. By 1850, Georgia had 36 cotton factories in operation; one year later four more factories were built and consumed 45,000 bales of cotton. Cotton was *King of the South* and Georgia the *Empire State of the South*.

ROSWELL MANUFACTURING COMPANY DAM

The 30 foot dam was built with massive timbers stacked with layers of rock, debris and earth, until it became a water proof obstruction controlling Vickery Creek's flow. A gate was built to divert water from the dam into a long structure called a millrace, which allowed the water to flow to the mill's overshot water wheel. The water became the power that turned the massive waterwheel.

RMC Mill Dam, author's photograph

THOMAS AND JAMES KING MILL

The Ivy Mill established in 1857 by the King brothers was a separate enterprise from the RMC. In 1864, the Ivy Mill factory was completely burned by the Union troops. After the war ended in 1865, a new mill was built beside the original Ivy Mill site. Empire Mills purchased Ivy Mill in 1871; Laurel Mills bought out Empire mills six years later. When the Georgia Power Company built the Morgan Falls Dam in 1904, it caused continuous flooding and damage to the mill and its equipment. The mill was abandoned in 1916, and the machinery was sold.

LEBANON MILL

There was a mill in 1819 on Vickery Creek built by Charles Wolford who was half-Cherokee. This mill existed when Roswell King arrived in north Georgia. It is very possible that King saw this mill operating since it was along the only road into the area, according to historian Michael Hitt and the 1832 area map. This mill was later sold to the Howell brothers who changed its name to the Lebanon mill. RMC bought that mill in 1844.

ANOTHER FACTORY IN ROSWELL

J.H. "Poney" Waller's Oxbow Manufacturing Company established a cotton mill on Oxbow Creek and Oxbow Road about 1894-96. (Oxbow was later changed to Oxbo). The mill used water from Hog Waller Creek to power its looms. When electricity replaced water as the predominant (and more economical) power source, the Oxbow Manufacturing Company did not have the money to refit and closed in 1913.

The Oxbow Falls Manufacturing Company also opened a mill called "The Pants Factory." It operated until its destruction by fire in 1941; a new building was constructed in 1942 on Hill Street, where the present day Roswell Police Department is located. The Pants Factory operated until 1975 with two hundred employees.

MILLWORKERS AND OCCUPATIONAL HAZARDS

A modern study of cotton mill workers done in 2010 (Indian Journal of Occupational and Environmental Medicine) states that respiratory diseases are due to inflammation and allergic reaction to cotton dust particles, inhaled during the manufacturing of cotton yarn and cloth.

117

This can result in chronic bronchitis, bronchial asthma, upper respiratory infections, and Byssinosis (brown lung disease). Millworkers' blood revealed a high level of eosinophils as a result of an allergic reaction to the dust. Measures to prevent these diseases include the following: workers should stop smoking tobacco products, management should provide education for workers, and enforce the use of personal protective devices such as masks and respirators at the work site.

Byssinosis, brown lung disease or Monday's disease, was worse at the beginning of the work week. Symptoms are chronic cough, wheezing, and chest tightness. Continued exposure can lead to decreased lung function, disability, and death.

Part 5 Union Occupation of Roswell, Georgia

Many historians have written about Sherman's Atlanta Campaign of 1864. Few of them mention what happened when Union troops came to the small Southern mill town of Roswell. Water was the lifeblood of the Roswell mills. The necessity of finding a way to cross that same river brought Federal forces to Roswell.

The following is a summary of events that led up to July 1864's military encounter at Roswell, Georgia; it is based on the letters and orders found in the *War of the Rebellion Official Records of the Union Army and the Confederate Army* and from Michael Hitt's book, *Charged With Treason: Ordeal of 400 MillWorkers During Military Operations in Roswell, Georgia, 1864-1865*. We owe him a great deal of thanks for his excellent research and dedication to learning the truth.

Preparing For The Worse

Barrington King received word of approaching Union armies on May 30, 1864, as General Johnson crossed the Etowah River. King decided to evacuate his family to Savannah; he would escape to Atlanta, taking along the books and papers of Roswell Manufacturing Company. King still had a few duties to perform as President of RMC before he could leave Roswell.

King could not remove the mills' machinery, but left instructions for Mr. Olney Eldridge, superintendent. Eldridge was to keep the mills operating and send off all the yarn to Atlanta immediately as it was produced. King ordered two months worth of provisions to be given to the RMC workers in case of a raid, or if they were captured by an approaching army. King also arranged to have hundreds of bales of cotton, yarn, and one thousand yards of cloth shipped to storage houses in Augusta, Newnan, Griffin, and Macon. He bought a house in Atlanta and packed up special pieces of Barrington Hall furniture to be stored there.

After seeing to all of these details, King left Atlanta to join his family, who had been sent to stay with his son Charles in Savannah. Charles was the pastor of White Bluff Congregational Church near Savannah at that time.

All of the founding families fled but one remained in Roswell (Pratts). Some arranged for their slaves to stay, but many like Barrington King sent their slaves to Macon, away from the Yankee invaders. Reverend Pratt and his family stayed at the Pratt house during the occupation. The Smith family evacuated their home and fled to Valdosta. The Hands had already moved in 1844, and George Camp was living at Primrose Cottage. He would escape with the Roswell Battalion. The Dunwodys had previously died, and their sons were fighting for the Confederacy.

Thomas King's widow, who was renting Bulloch Hall from Martha Bulloch in New York City, was instructed to leave. Mrs. Thomas King spoke with Theophile Roche' asking him to look after Bulloch Hall. Roche' was a weaver at Ivy Mill's Woolen factory, but was also the French tutor of both the King and Smith's children.

Captain James R. King prepared his woolen mill for the rumored raid. All male and female workers were to remain to protect the property; these instructions were given to Samuel Bonfoy, Ivy Mill's superintendent.

South to Atlanta

Major General William T. Sherman had one objective, to take the war home to the South and pressure the civilians to demand an end. His campaign from Dalton to Kennesaw Mountain was a series of flanking maneuvers with corresponding retreating by General Joe Johnson's Confederate forces.

While Sherman's army was occupied at Kennesaw Mountain, the Georgia state troops under General G.W. Smith were ordered on June 12th to guard the Chattahoochee River Bridge, located at Roswell. The bridge was ordered to be burned, if it could no longer be defended. By July 1st, only the Roswell Battalion remained to guard the Roswell factories and bridge. Captain James R. King and Private George Camp defended the town and the bridge along with the Roswell Battalion. With news of the evacuation of Kennesaw Mountain and Marietta, the Roswell residents' fears of an expected raid were realized.

Major General George Thomas and the Union Army of the Cumberland advanced into Marietta; Generals McPherson and Schofield continued southward along the Sandtown Road. Union troops were attempting to flank the Confederates, but they met strong opposition in early July. General Johnston had the Chattahoochee River behind him now. Sherman decided to pull Schofield's army out of line, and send it back to Smyrna to be held in reserve, ready to cross the river.

General Johnston fortified two defensive lines beyond Kennesaw Mountain outside of the Chattahoochee River. Major General Sherman advanced to set up headquarters, first at Smyrna and then Vinings. Seeing the strong defensive situation of the Confederates, Sherman refused to do a frontal attack. Instead, he tried to outflank Johnston again and needed to find several river crossings to advance Union troops over the Chattahoochee River northeast of Johnston. Spring was ending and the rushing waters from the north Georgia mountains were beginning to decrease, the water level of the Chattahoochee River was starting to recede.

Roswell, The Staging Area For Assault On Atlanta

Sherman ordered General Garrard to go to Roswell on July 4th to stop the Confederates' attempts to sabotage Union troop communications. Garrard was also to arrest all citizens who were likely spies for the Confederacy. Sherman's objective was to keep communications and the Union held Western and Atlantic Railroad free from attack.

Sherman was aware of how important Roswell's factories were to the Confederate forces. Sherman also knew Roswell had a bridge over the Chattahoochee River, which would allow Union troops easy access to advance on Atlanta. If the Confederate Calvary were allowed to cross the river, Garrard was to oppose and control that force.

Garrard was also to send couriers to communicate with Sherman and send soldiers along the railroad, which could be threatened by the Confederate forces. General Sherman was concerned that General Joe Wheeler's Confederate troops would inflict damage to the railroad between Marietta and Allatoona, which would interfere with the Union's supply lines.

General Garrard left early for Roswell along with troops from Pennsylvania, Ohio, Illinois, Indiana, and Michigan. The 7th Pennsylvania was Garrard's advance guard. Upon arrival in Roswell on July 5th, Garrard initially had no direct orders to burn the mills, and so he allowed them to continue to operate.

The Confederates fled across the Chattahoochee River; Roswell was now left with only the Roswell Battalion to defend the town, mills, and people. The Roswell Battalion held out as long as possible and left Roswell at 11 AM on July 5th and crossed the covered bridge over the Chattahoochee River. Captain James King followed the order to burn the bridge as the 7th Pennsylvania Cavalry rode along Azalea Road (present day name). The weather was extremely hot, and the three Union brigades found rest as they approached Roswell (by Georgia Route 120). The 7th Pennsylvania Calvary rested three days along Willeo Creek. Some of the 72nd Indiana infantry located blackberries and enjoyed the feast immensely.

When the 72th Pennsylvania Cavalry finally arrived, they found the bridge burned. The officers noticed the woolen mill, located near the bridge, seemed alive with women and children.

The officers approached the superintendent of the Ivy Mill, Samuel Bonfoy. They asked why the millworkers continued to operate the mill machinery. Bonfoy stated that they were subjects of Great Britain and France. A French flag was flying over the mill. Therefore, the mill was neutral and under the protection of these nations. (A French flag was also thought flying over Bulloch Hall).

Word was sent to Garrard who decided to personally visit the mill site to ascertain if the claim of neutrality was valid. As the workers continued to make the heavy cloth, Garrard noticed CSA woven on a completed bolt. He ordered the French flag removed from the mill, removed the mill's private papers, and notified all workers to immediately leave the building. Both Bonfoy and Roche', a weaver, refused and a Union guard was ordered to physically remove them. The mill's papers were sent to army headquarters now located at Barrington Hall.

Garrard sent two inspectors to the RMC mills and communicated to General Sherman that the mills remained operational and were making goods for the Confederacy. Garrard ordered all millworkers to leave RMC mills, return home, gather their belongings, and return within two hours to the village square. Garrard had already intended to destroy all factory buildings, paper mills, and machine shops. The Union troops gathered the cotton cloth from the RMC mills and sent it back to the Marietta Union hospitals; they gave some of the cloth to the millworkers as they left the mills.

Burning of Mills and Charged With Treason

Meantime, Garrard gave the feared order on July 6ᵗʰ to burn all of the mills in Roswell; after this was accomplished, he summarized his actions and related to General Sherman that there were several possible crossings for the troops. The last mill burned itself out by the night of July 6ᵗʰ. The Union troops eventually burned fifteen buildings.

On July 7ᵗʰ, Sherman heard about the destruction of the mills and was quite pleased. He was surprised that the mills were still operating. He gave orders to Garrard to charge employees and owners of the mills with treason because, they were openly hostile to our government by laboring and supplying the enemies' armies. He reiterated that all males, females, and their children connected to the factories were to be arrested, sent by foot to Marietta under guard, and then sent by rail cars to the north. His famous statement recorded for all future Southerners to read, "The poor women will make a howl" will forever be interpreted as callous and unnecessary.

General Sherman based his action to charge them with treason on General Order #100 from the Federal War Department, which stated: *Armed or unarmed resistance by citizens of the United States against the lawful movements of their troops is levying war against the Untied States and is therefore Treason.*

General Garrard carried out Sherman's orders and no official civilian or military trials were held to determine guilt or innocence. Once the millworkers were assembled, they were detained at the square. Garrard then moved his troops to the middle of town to camp on July 8th. General Joe Wheeler's troops were camped across the river and reported the Union activity. The 4th Ohio Volunteer Cavalry was ordered to hold McAfee Bridge and prevent Confederates from crossing over. McAfee Bridge was located east of Roswell on the Chattahoochee River. It too will be a crossing site for Union troops.

Once camped in Roswell, the Union surgeons designated a hospital to be set up in the Presbyterian Church. The extremely high temperatures in July resulted in heat exhaustion in as many as twenty Union soldiers. Two deaths were recorded due to sunstroke. The surgeons were giving whiskey and laudanum to the sunstroke victims, which no doubt hastened their dehydration and death.

The only military action that took place in Roswell was on July 9th at 3 AM when the 17th and 72nd Indiana, and the 98th and 123rd Illinois skirmished with Wheeler's Cavalry over the river, near the southern end of Atlanta Street. The Union troops were successful at driving the Confederates away without injury, and word was sent to Sherman that the site was safe to ford.

Major General John A. Dodge arrived in Roswell with his engineering force to build a floating bridge across the Chattahoochee River. A soldier from the 48th Illinois drowned while crossing the bridge and four of Dodge's scouts were captured by rebel cavalry at Alpharetta. General Dodge was remembered for an act of kindness toward the arrested women. He sent word to Surgeon Aston of the 7th Iowa in charge of Marietta hospitals to hire as many of the female millworkers as possible and pay them along with rations to nurse Union soldiers.

On July 10th, the millworkers were sent from Roswell by wagon and horseback and arrived at the Georgia Military Institute (GMI) in Marietta. They were housed along with the workers from New Manchester Factory on Sweetwater Creek. William King, brother of Barrington King, visited the millworkers at GMI who were waiting for transport out of Georgia by rail to Tennessee. He documented their plight in his diary.

General Sherman sent a message to General Webster in Nashville, Tennessee. He warned that when the millworkers from Roswell and Sweetwater arrived, to "send them across the Ohio River where they cannot do any harm to us".

Back in Roswell by July 14th, Major General James McPherson arrived and set up his headquarters with General Dodge at Ivy Mill. Dodge had recently completed the pole bridge across the Chattahoochee River; McPherson sent his XV Corps across the bridge that afternoon. General Garrard moved his cavalry and the Chicago Board of Trade Battery to Newtown, where Old Alabama and Nesbit Ferry Road intersect to cross over McAfee's Bridge.

A Storm Strikes

During the second week of July, the weather suddenly changed as a typical Southern storm advanced along the path of the Chattahoochee River in the evening. There was little rain, but high winds and a fierce electrical storm attacked the troops camped around Roswell. Michael Hitt records the words of a soldier, James Snell, who stated that the storm caused the death of one Negro and one white soldier from the Pioneer Corps. Two men were killed and eleven wounded from the 18th Mounted Infantry Volunteers, and two men wounded from the division. One horse and one soldier were injured at Dodge's headquarters (Pratt's house), and three mules were lost from another pioneer unit. Three men of the 2nd U.S. Artillery of the 4th Division were killed instantly.

No doubt the deaths were due to lightening strikes; another soldier recorded that a tree fell on a group of men from the 2nd U.S. Artillery, killing them instantly. Surgeon John Moore added his comment that thirty or more men were (temporarily) paralyzed and stacked guns struck by lightening were destroyed. The men who were killed would eventually find their rest at Marietta's Georgia National Cemetery.

As the regiments moved forward, McPherson ordered guards to patrol the vicinity around Roswell, to prevent being surprised by the enemy. Although Roswell was under Union occupation for three weeks, there was continuous movement through the area and town over the next several weeks. (Some writers claim the Union presence lasted several months).

By July 17th, General John Bell Hood replaced General Johnston as commander of the Confederate defenders of Atlanta. In Roswell, the XVII Union Army Corps marched through Roswell attempting to catch up to McPherson's Corps. Confederate scouts lurking near Roswell reported this activity to General Hood.

Attacks Surrounding Atlanta

The Battle of Peachtree Creek commenced on July 20th, the first defeat for Hood. Two days later on July 22nd, the Battle of Atlanta was fought east of the city, and Hood again was defeated. The Battle of Ezra Church on July 28th was another blow to the Confederates.

During early August, Sherman maintained Federal authority over Roswell and its bridges even as the Confederates attempted to raid the Federal supply trains. Sherman removed his guards from Roswell on August 6th. He declared that Roswell was of no great importance, and ordered the temporary Roswell

Bridge to be burned. On August 7th, Brigadier-General John McArthur destroyed the bridge; the Chattahoochee River was easily forded with the drop in the water level. The McAfee Bridge remained guarded by Federal cavalry to cover the back door of the Union forces.

Captain James King, commander the Roswell Battalion, was captured on August 20th by the 1st brigade 2nd Cavalry Division at Macon, Georgia. James was a Union prisoner of war.

By August 26th, Confederate troops had arrived in Roswell, and it became the base for the Confederate Cavalry under Colonel Minty. Roswell civilians were not permitted to travel in or out of Roswell.

News arrived that Hood was defeated at the Battle of Jonesboro (August 31th-September 1st). Confederate deserters fleeing to the Union Army were rounded up and shipped north. Confederate soldiers were warned that if any soldier left Hood's Army to take the "oath", Confederate scouts would hang them if caught. Reverend Pratt wrote that deserting Confederate soldiers were causing havoc in Roswell by stealing, plundering, and vandalizing the properties.

On September 2nd, Atlanta fell to Sherman's XX Corps; General Garrard's units continued to guard the vicinity around Roswell. By October 1st, all Federal troops were gone from Roswell except for the 9th Michigan Cavalry; it patrolled Roswell from the Decatur Camp. While on patrol, several members of the Roswell Battalion were captured. The men were sent to military prison in Louisville, Kentucky, and some to Camp Douglas in Chicago. Second Lieutenant Minhinnett, being an officer, was sent to Johnson's Island prison on an island in Sandusky Bay, Ohio.

Union troops left Roswell as General Sherman's forces evacuated Atlanta and began the *March to the Sea*. More deserters arrived and caused even more havoc. It was not until May 20,

1865, that the remaining Roswell Battalion surrendered to Federal authorities in Augusta, Georgia, and took the oath of allegiance.

Roswell Refugees

The end of the journey for the millworkers who were sent north from Roswell was now in sight. The Roswell and Sweetwater millworkers arrived by rail in Kentucky on about July 20th. The Roswell women and children were marched to a military prison, which was a Louisville hospital; but it was so overcrowded that another house was added at Broadway and 12th Street to accommodate the prisoners.

Many residents of Louisville were concerned over the refugees' welfare. The prisoners lacked proper food and medical attention. Some women who had been released by the military lacked any form of shelter or means to pay for food or clothing.

As a result, a Commission For The Aid of Refugees was formed to educate the public of these conditions. The town was filled with over one thousand refugees (women, children and even men) from various Southern towns. The Commission members made it their duty to provide for the refugees and obtain housing, proper food, and clothing before the coming winter season. The refugee children were described as living skeletons, whole families were living in one room in the military prison.

On September 22nd, the Assistant Surgeon General of the Union Medical Department assigned a female surgeon, Dr. Mary Walker, to Louisville to treat the female refugees and their children, who were dying of typhoid fever. Dr. Walker and the refugees did not get along, and soon the refugees rebelled. The Commission sent complaints to Dr. Walker's superior, Lt. Col. Thomas Farleigh. Dr. Walker defended her actions, but was relieved from duty on March 22, 1865.

On February 23, 1865, the millworkers remaining in Louisville's prison were finally freed. Some of the millworkers found employment as servants to various families in the area; some of the skilled workers found employment at the cotton mill at Cannelton, Indiana. Cannelton is located southwest of Louisville along the Ohio River. The Cannelton mill faced the Ohio River on the northern bank (Indiana).

Those Roswell millworkers, who wanted to go home, did not arrive in Roswell until July 1865. The majority of Roswell's arrested millworkers never returned to Roswell; some of them married and remained in Kentucky or Indiana, a few died from age or harsh living conditions, and others found gainful employment in northern mills. One writer estimated that about twenty workers returned, but only a few found employment in Roswell.

Millworkers Memorial

The Roswell Mills Camp #1547 Sons of Confederate Veterans remembered the Lost Millworkers of Roswell on July 8, 2000. A ten-foot granite monument was installed at the east end of Old Mill Park on Sloan Street. The Roswell King Monument in Founders Cemetery inspired the Monument of Honor. This memorial was a gift to the City of Roswell. The inscription reads *Honoring the memory of the four hundred women, children and men millworkers of Roswell who were charged with treason and deported by train to the North by invading Federal forces July 10, 1864.*

Roswell's Aftermath

Reverend Nathaniel A. Pratt was witness to the behavior of Union troops, Confederate deserters, and unrestrained civilians. He wrote to his nephew, Colonel Barrington S. King, in December 1864, and related the following information.

The Monument of Honor by Roswell Mill Camp SCV 2000,
author's photograph

Pratt's house and grounds were totally used by the Union troops. Over one thousand wagons and six thousand mules and horses were stabled on the lush grounds. Tents and stores of supplies were unloaded reaching to the front door. Pratt's highly productive farm was robbed of 30 acres of corn, 60-70 bushels of wheat, and 7 acres of sorghum; all were destroyed or harvested for use by the army. General Vetch was quite ill and found quarters in Pratt's house along with General Jonathan "Black Jack" Logan.

Some of the other mansions fared better. General Garrard used Barrington Hall as his headquarters during the occupation. Wandering families moved into each room of the house after the Union Army left. Ivy Mill and RMC had hidden $60-75,000 worth of copper but some was located and stolen by locals.

The immediate problem was the returning Confederate soldiers, who were starving, and also those who were deserting. They were stealing horses and mules from the starving wives of Roswell soldiers and poor widows of the Confederate dead.

I WANT TO KNOW MORE ABOUT:

TIMELINE OF EVENTS OF THE UNION OCCUPATION
    1864-1865
1864:

May 30   Barrington King left Roswell and stayed in Atlanta (later Savannah)

June 27   Battle of Kennesaw Mountain

July 1   500 men at Shallowford guarded the Roswell Bridge

July 3   Marietta evacuated, Ralph King & Mrs. Thomas King left for Macon

July 5-6	The Roswell Bridge was burned. General Garrard arrived in Roswell & burned the mills. All of the mills totally burned (15 buildings).
July 7&8	Roswell millworkers, who gathered at the square, were arrested.
July 9	Skirmish at the river at the end of Atlanta Street
July 10-12	Millworkers arrived at GMI in Marietta
July 20	Millworkers started to arrive at new army hospital in the female military prison, Louisville, Kentucky
Aug. 7	Millworkers held at new army hospital in Louisville, KY
Aug. 10	Women sent to female military prison
Sept. 2	Atlanta fell to Federal forces
Sept. 22	Dr. Walker sent to care for female millworkers at the prison
Nov. 12	Sherman began March to the Sea

1865:

Jan	Dr. Walker relieved of duty
Feb 23	Female millworkers released from Louisville prison
April 9	Lee surrendered and President Lincoln's amnesty proclamation announced
July	Some millworkers returned to Roswell

ROSWELL GUARDS

The Roswell Guards or Company H of Cobb County were one of nine companies that formed the Georgia 7th Infantry Regiment, in May 1861 at Atlanta. Their first assignment was at Harpers Ferry, Virginia, in June 1861, under Colonel F.S. Bartows Brigade, Army of the Shenandoah. The 7th served under the command of General G. T. Anderson and the Army of Northern Virginia throughout the war. The Guard participated in the following battles: First Manassas, Yorktown, New Bridge, Seven Days, Cold Harbor, Rappahannock Station, Second Manassas, Sharpsburg, Fredericksburg, Suffolk, Gettysburg, Funkstown, Charleston, Chattanooga, Knoxville, Wilderness, Petersburg, and Appomattox.

The Roswell Guard Flag: Fanny King, James R. King's wife cut up her crimson crape shawl; Marie, wife of Thomas King, supplied white satin and blue silk from two dresses. The flag had big white silk lettering R G and eleven silken stars on a blue silk field.

Lt. Colonel John Dunwody from Roswell was an officer with Roswell Guards.

ROSWELL BATTALION

Organized on June 28, 1863, this company was created for home defense to protect land north of Atlanta to the Alabama and Tennessee lines. Their purpose was to repel a Yankee raid. A good portion was composed of men who worked for the Confederate State Government under Major G.W. Cunningham, Quarter Master for Atlanta at Roswell Factories. It consisted of men and boys from 16 to 60 years of age. It was originally a battalion of infantry, cavalry, and artillery, composed principally of men who operated the cotton and woolen mills at Roswell.

Once the Confederates evacuated Marietta, many of these men deserted. The rest were ordered to mount and burn the Roswell bridge on July 5, 1864. On December 31, 1864, the Roswell Battalion merged with the 24th Alabama Cavalry Battalion Co. B and Co. A Georgia; and later merged with the 53rd Alabama Cavalry Regiment, Partisan Rangers. All three cavalry units served in the Army of Tennessee with

General Joseph Wheeler's Cavalry Corps. They fought in the Atlanta Campaign and the Carolinas Campaign. They were paroled May 8, 1965, in Augusta, Georgia, by orders from Colonel Moses Wright Hannon.

Thomas E. King was elected captain of the battalion. Other founding sons on the original roster were Captain Charles A. Dunwody, Captain James R. King, 1st Lt. Joseph H. King, 1st Lt. Ralph B. King, 1st Lt. Charles Pratt Jr., Private George H. Camp, and Private William Pratt.

Conclusion

The founding families of the Colony of Roswell were deeply rooted in this country's birth. Their ancestors arrived in the British Colonies to build a new life. Many of the descendants' fathers fought in the War for Independence, and some fought against the British in the War of 1812. Each family had one or more sons who fought for the Confederacy in the American Civil War. The patriotic spirit ran through each generation. Their heritage was built on men and women who pioneered this new world; it is no wonder that the same spirit of adventure brought their descendants to the foothills of the Applachian Mountains in north Georgia.

The Town of Roswell was incorporated on February 16, 1854. Today, Roswell is the eighth largest city in Georgia with a population of 88,345 according to the United States Census of 2010. Once only one square mile, the Roswell City limit has expanded to forty square miles located within Fulton County.

Roswell is a commuter's city twenty miles north of Atlanta. It has thirteen parks with nine hundred acres of parkland and facilities. The average household income is $135,186.00. Roswell residents enjoy a suburban country lifestyle with several golf course communities, pool and tennis subdivisions, excellent school districts, many shopping boutiques, quaint restaurants, and friendly people.

Roswell King would be pleased.

Appendix

Figures 1,2,3,4, Barrington King's letter asking to become a citizen again August 1865

Figures 5,6,7, Captain James R. King letter petitioning for pardon after the war September 1865

Figure 8, Andrew Johnson's May 1865 Amnesty

Proclamation

Figure 1

Georgia   To His Excellency
Cobb County   Andrew Johnson
President of the United States of America.

     The petition of Barrington King
a citizen of and for twenty seven years
past a constant resident of said County
most respectfully shews unto Your
Excellency
1st. That he is sixty seven years of age —
five feet eleven inches high — fair Complexion,
hair grey and eyes blue and a Native
of Darien Georgia, and by occupation
a cotton Manufacturer —
2d. That he has never held any office
in his life Civil or Military, having
devoted his whole life to business —
That being over age he took no part
in the rebellion except as did almost
every man in the State by donations
of food and clothing to the hungry
and naked whether in or out of the
army — this much he deemed due
to our common humanity —
That he has been all his life profoundly
attached to the Union of the States and
was opposed to secession, but when
by almost a unanimous vote the
Convention of his native State passed
the Ordinance of Secession, he
accepted and acquiesced in it —
3. That on the 26th day of April

140

Figure 2

last he took the Oath of Amnesty under President Lincoln's Proclamation, which was as early an opportunity as he had of doing so —

4th. He distinctly states that he would be enabled now to take the Oath prescribed by Your Excellency in Your Proclamation of the 29th May 1865 and thereby avail himself of Your Excellency's Clemency, were it not for the fact that his taxable property is worth in his judgement exceeding twenty thousand dollars, and he is therefore precluded from that privilege —

5th. He also distinctly states that he does not fall within any of the other exceptions made in Your Excellency's said Proclamation — And that the Government of the United States has not taken possession of any of his property so far as he knows, has heard or believes — That no proceedings whatever have been instituted against him for treason or for Conspiracy against the Government of the United States or for any other cause whatever —

6th. That his property consists of stock in the Roswell Manufacturing Company and other stocks in Georgia, real estate in Town and Country all in the State of Georgia and a

Figure 3

small lot of Cotton – he deems the whole
worth about one hundred thousand
dollars – he does not suppose it could
be sold for that sum now, but thinks
it well worth that sum –

7th The premises considered your
petitioner most respectfully but
earnestly prays Your Excellency to
grant him a special pardon and
restore him to his rights & privileges
as a citizen of the United States –
That he has this day taken the oath
prescribed in Your Excellency's said
Proclamation, which is hereto annexed
as a part of his petition, and that he
will to the utmost of his ability
faithfully fulfill and discharge all
his duties and obligations as a true
and loyal citizen of the United
States – And as in duty bound he
will ever pray &c
August 23: 1865   B. King

Georgia
Cobb County } Before me in person
came Barrington King the petitioner
who being duly sworn says, that the
foregoing petition is true in substance
and in fact –

Sworn to & subscribed
before me this 23
day of August 1865
Nols Campbell   B. King
Ord'inans C C

142

Figure 4

Cook County
came Barrington King the petitioner
who being duly sworn says, that the
foregoing petition is true in substance
and in fact

Sworn to & subscribed
before me this 23d 1865

R. S. King

United States of America.

GEORGIA,
    Cobb County.

I do solemnly swear, or affirm, in the presence of Almighty God, that I will henceforth faithfully SUPPORT, PROTECT, AND DEFEND the Constitution of the United States and the union of the States thereunder, and that I will, in like manner, ABIDE BY AND FAITHFULLY SUPPORT ALL LAWS AND PROCLAMATIONS which have been made during the existing rebellion, with reference ... tion of slaves—SO HELP ME GOD.

143

Figure 5

State Georgia
Chatham County

To His Excellency Andy Johnson
President of the United States.

Having taking the Oath of allegiance
presented by Pres.t Lincolns proclamation
of the 8th Dec 1863 I desire to enjoy the
rights and privileges of Citizenship in
accordance with the amnesty Oath prescribed by the Presidents proclamation
of May 9th 1865.

In this My petition for pardon I would
respectfully state. that in the march of
the federal army through Georgia the most
of my property was destroyed. tho I may
get fall under the 13th Exception, I
was Engaged in woolen Manufg being detaild
and have in My Employ detailed operations the products of the Mill were
appropriated by the Confederate Government

After the destruction of Said Mills
by Gen Sherman I entered Service as
Capt of Cavalry—

The Government has not token possession
of any part of My property. nor has
any action been had against me in
the Courts for treason or otherwise

144

Figure 6

In view of the above facts I respectful[ly]
petition the Executive clemency having
fully and truly complied with the
requisitions of his Excellency Pres[identia]l
Johnson as set forth in his proclamati[on]
of 9ᵗʰ May 1865

And your petitioner will ever
pray &c   James. R. King

State Georgia
Chatham County

Appeared James R King who being
duly Sworn declares that the Statement
as set forth in the foregoing petition are true
Sworn to and Subscribed
before me at Savannah   James R King
this 3ᵈ Day of August
1866.

F.S. Coffin
Lieut &c Asst, Pro Mar

Figure 7

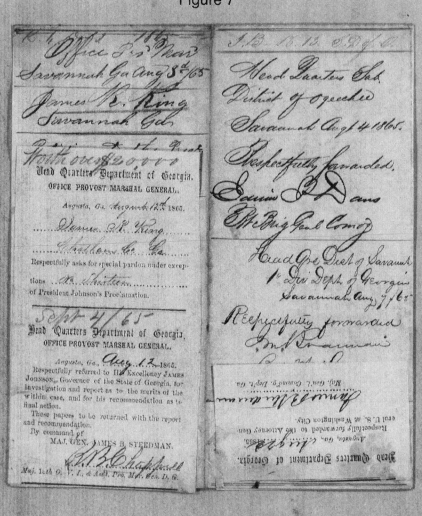

Figure 8
Amnesty Proclamation, Andrew Johnson - 29 May 1865

Whereas the President of the United States, on the 8th day of December, A.D. eighteen hundred and sixty-three, and on the 26 day of March, A.D. eighteen hundred and sixty-four, did, with the object to suppress the existing rebellion, to induce all persons to return to their loyalty, and to restore the authority of the United States, issue proclamations offering amnesty and pardon to certain persons who had directly or by implication participated in the said rebellion; and whereas many persons who had so engaged in said rebellion have, since the issuance of said proclamations, failed or neglected to take the benefits offered thereby; and whereas many persons who have been justly deprived of all claim to amnesty and pardon thereunder, by reason of their participation directly or by implication in said rebellion, and continued hostility to the government of the United States since the date of said proclamation, now desire to apply for and obtain amnesty and pardon:

To the end, therefore, that the authority of the government of the United States may be restored, and that peace, order, and freedom may be established, I, ANDREW JOHNSON, President of the United States, do proclaim and declare that I hereby grant to all persons who have, directly or indirectly, participated in the existing rebellion, except as hereinafter excepted, amnesty and pardon, with restoration of all rights of property, except as to slaves, and except in cases where legal proceedings, under the laws of the United States providing for the confiscation of property of persons engaged in rebellion, have been instituted; but upon the condition, nevertheless, that every such person shall take and subscribe the following oath, (or affirmation,) and thenceforward keep and maintain said oath inviolate; and which oath shall be registered for permanent preservation, and shall be of the tenor and effect following, to wit:

I,_____, do solemnly swear, (or affirm,) in presence of Almighty God, that I will henceforth faithfully support, protect, and defend the Constitution of the United States, and the union of the States thereunder; and that I will, in like manner, abide by, and faithfully support all laws and proclamations which have been made during the existing rebellion with reference to the emancipation of slaves. So help me God.

The following classes of persons are excepted from the benefits of this proclamation: 1st, all who are or shall have been pretended civil or diplomatic officers or otherwise domestic or foreign agents of the pretended Confederate government; 2nd, all who left judicial stations under the United States to aid the rebellion; 3d, all who shall have been military or naval officers of said pretended Confederate government above the rank of colonel in the army or lieutenant in the navy; 4th, all who left seats in the Congress of the United States to aid the rebellion; 5th, all who resigned or tendered resignations of their commissions in the army or navy of the United States to evade duty in resisting the rebellion; 6th, all who have engaged in any way in treating otherwise than lawfully as prisoners of war persons found in the United States service, as officers, soldiers, seamen, or in other capacities; 7th, all persons who have been, or are absentees from the United States for the purpose of aiding the rebellion; 8th, all military and naval officers in the rebel service, who were educated by the government in the Military Academy at West Point or the United States Naval Academy; 9th, all persons who held the pretended offices of governors of States in insurrection against the United States; 10th, all persons who left their homes within the jurisdiction and protection of the United States, and passed beyond the Federal military lines into the pretended Confederate States for the purpose of aiding the rebellion; 11th, all persons who have been engaged in the destruction of the commerce of the United States upon the high seas, and all persons who have made raids into the United States from Canada, or been engaged in destroying the commerce of the United States upon the lakes and rivers that separate the British Provinces from the United States; 12th, all persons who, at the time when they seek to obtain the benefits hereof by taking the oath herein prescribed, are in military, naval, or civil confinement, or custody, or under bonds of the civil, military, or naval authorities, or agents of the United States as prisoners of war, or persons detained for offenses of any kind, either before or after conviction; 13th, all persons who have voluntarily participated in said rebellion, and the estimated value of whose taxable property is over twenty thousand dollars; 14th, all persons who have taken the oath of amnesty as prescribed in the President's proclamation of December 8th, A.D. 1863, or an oath of allegiance to the government of the United States since the date of said proclamation, and who have not thenceforward kept and maintained the same inviolate.

Provided, That special application may be made to the President for pardon by any person belonging to the excepted classes; and such clemency will be liberally extended as may be consistent with the facts of the case and the peace and dignity of the United States.

The Secretary of State will establish rules and regulations for administering and recording the said amnesty oath, so as to insure its benefit to the people, and guard the government against fraud.

In testimony where of, I have here unto set my hand, and caused the seal of the United States to be affixed.

Done at the City of Washington, the twenty-ninth day of May, in the year of our Lord one thousand eight hundred and sixty-five, and of the Independence of the United States the eighty-ninth.

ANDREW JOHNSON

By the President:
WILLIAM H. SEWARD, Secretary of State

Bibliography

Books

Ambrose, Andy. *An Illustrated History*. Atlanta: Hillstreet Press, 2003

Bell, Malcolm Jr. *Major Butler's Legacy Five Generations of A Slaveholding Family*. Athens: University of Georgia Press, 1987

Bulloch, Joseph Gaston Baillie, Dr. *A History and Genealogy of The Habersham Family*. Columbia, South Carolina: R. L. Bryan Co., 1901

A History and Genealogy of The Families of Bulloch and Stobo and of Irvine Cults, 1911

Bulloch, Donald, Ian. *The Bullochs of Baldernock 1591-2001*. Perth, Western Australia: D.I. Bulloch, self published, 2014.

Caroli, Betty Boyd. *The Roosevelt Women*. New York: Basic Books, 1998

Canfield, Cars. *The Iron Will of Jefferson Davis*. New York: Harcourt Brace Jovanovich, 1978

Clarke, Erskine. *Dwelling Place A Plantation Epic*. New Haven: Yale University, 2005

Coleman, Kenneth. *A History of Georgia*. Athens: University of Georgia Press, 1977

Fraser, Walter J. *Savannah In The Old South*. Athens: University of Georgia Press, 2005

Gallay, Alan. *The Formation of A Planter Elite*. Athens: University of Georgia Press, 2007

Galloway, Tammy Harden. *Dear Old Roswell*. Macon: Mercer University Press, 2003

Granger, Mary, editor. *Savannah River Plantations*. Savannah: Oglethorpe Press Inc., 1997

Groover, Robert Long. *Sweet Land of Liberty: A History of Liberty Co. GA*. Georgia: Wolfe Assoc., 1987

Hitt, Michael. Charged *With Treason: Ordeal of 400 Mill Workers During Military Operations In Roswell, Georgia*. Monroe, New York: Library Research Associates, 1992

Jackson, Skakey, Herbury et. al. *The Georgia Studies Book Our State and Nation*. Athens: University Press, 2001

Johoda, Gloria. *The Trail of Tears: The Story of The American Indian Removals*. New York: Wing Books, 1975

Jeffrey, A. *The History And Antiquities of Roxburghshire and Adjacent Districts From The Most remote Period To The Present Time*. London, Edinburgh: Vol.4, 1855-64

King, Spencer, B. Jr. *Darien: The Death and Rebirth of A Southern Town*. Macon: Mercer University Press, 1981

Lawson, Sherron. *A Guide To The Historic Textile Mill Town of Roswell, Georgia*. Roswell: Roswell Historical Society, 1996.

Lodge, John and Archdall, Mervyn. *The Peerage of Ireland* Dublin: James Moore, Vol. I & II, 1789

Marye, Florence. Georgia's Early Gardens 1566-1865. Atlanta: Peachtree Garden Club, 1933

McCullough, David. *Mornings On HorseBack*. New York: Simon and Schuster, 2000

McMurry, Richard M. Atlanta 1864: *Last chance for the Confederacy*. Kansas: University of Nebraska. Bison Books, 2000

Mosley, Charles. *Burke's Peerage, Baronetage and Knightage: Clans Chiefs, Scottish Feudal Lords*. London: Burke's Peerage and Gentry, Vol. 1, 2003

Myers, Robert Manson. *The Children Of Pride (unabridged)*. New Haven: Yale University Press, 1972

Nirenstein, Virginia King. *With Kindly Voices: A Nineteenth-Century Georgia Family*. Macon: Tullous Books, 1984

Roswell Presbyterian Church. *A History of The Roswell Presbyterian Church. 1st. ed.* allas: Taylor Publishing, 1984

Skinner, Arthur. *The Death of A Confederate*. Athens: University of Georgia Press, 1996

Skinner, James L. *The Refugees of Roswell*. Roswell, Georgia: Roswell Historical Society, 2004

Trimpi, Helen. *Crimson Confederates: Harvard Men Who Fought For The South*. Knoxville: University of Tennessee Press, 2009

Vanstory, Burnette. *Georgia's Land of The Golden Isles*. Athens: University of Georgia Press, 1981

Wilson, Walter and McKay, Gary. *James D. Bulloch: Secret Agent And Mastermind of The Confederate Navy*. Jefferson, N.C. and London: McFarland & Company, Inc. 2012

Journals and Newspapers

Dolvin, Emily. "Bulloch Hall and The Wing Family." *Old Atlanta,* Vol. 1, (1992)

Griffin, Richard. "The Origins of The Industrial Revolution In Georgia 1810-1865." *The Georgia Historical Quarterly,* Vol. 42, No. 4, (1958)

National Archives of The Presbyterian Church. *Journal of Presbyterian Historical Society.* XXXVII Vol. #3, Sept. (1959)

Roswell Archives. "The Reverend Nathaniel Pratt." Roswell Historical Society Newsletter. (unknown date)

Shylock, R.H. "The Early Industrial Revolution In The Empire State." *The Georgia Historical Quarterly.* Vol.11, No. 2, (1927)

Wood, Karen G. "Textile Mills Of Roswell Georgia." *Early Georgia* Vol. 21, No. 1 (1993)

Yeipude, Provin and Jogdana, Kerrti. "Morbidity Profile of Cotton Mill Workers". *Indian Journal of Occupational & Environmental Medicine.*Vol.14 issue 3, p. 94-96 (2010)

Pamphlets

Drake, Eleanor. "The Smiths of Roswell, Georgia", Roswell, GA: Roswell Historical Society Research Library Archives

Hitt, Michael D. "In Memory of Cemetery Records of Roswell, GA." Roswell: Roswell Historical Society Research Library Archives, 1994

Websites

"Ancestors of Rhea King." Family Tree Making Genealogy Sites, Ancestor.com, accessed Jan. 2015

Bettyboat@aol.com. "The Elliotts, Roosevelts and Liberty County GA." Rootsweb.com, accessed Jan. 2015

King, William. " Diary of William King, Cobb Co. Georgia" web accessed Dec. 2014

"Georgia's Land Lotteries." *About North Georgia*. Golden Ink: Woodstock, GA. 1998, accessed Dec. 2014

"The Scottish Ancestors of President Roosevelt". *The Scottish Historical Review: A Collection of Articles, Electricscotland.com* accessed February 2015

"The Internet Surname Database.", WWW.surnamedb.com/surname/barrington, accessed Nov. 2014

"The Internet Surname Database.", WWW.surnamedb.com/surname/bulloch, accessed Nov. 2014

"The Internet Surname Database." ,WWW.surnamedb.com/surname/elliott, accessed Nov. 2014

"The Internet Surname Database.", WWW.surnamedb.com/surname/fitch, accessed Nov. 2014

"The Internet Surname Database.", WWW.surnamedb.com/surname/hand, accessed Nov. 2014

"The Internet Surname Database.", WWW.surnamedb.com/surname/king, accessed Nov. 2014

"The Internet Surname Database.", WWW.surnamedb.com/surname/pratt, accessed Nov. 2014

"The Internet Surname Database.", WWW.surnamedb.com/surname/smith, accessed Nov. 2014

Primary Resources

"Confederate War Records of The Roswell Battalion 1863-1864", Morrow, Georgia: Georgia Dept. of Archives and History

"The King Collection.", Roswell: Roswell Historical Society Research Library Archives

"Letters of Archibald Smith Family." Morrow, GA: Georgia State Archives

"Letters of Bulloch Family." Savannah, GA: Georgia Historical Society

"Letters of Julia King Maxwell." Midway, GA: Midway Church Archives

"Letters of Nathaniel A. Pratt." Savannah, GA: Georgia Historical Society

"Minutes of The Roswell Manufacturing Company Stockholders 1840-1899." Roswell, GA: Roswell Historical Society Research Library and Archives

United States War Dept. "The War of the Rebellion: A Compilation of the Official Records of the Union and Confederate Armies (OR's)". Washington D.C.: Government Printing Office, 1881-1901: Series 1, Vol. 8; Series 1, Vol. 38 Pt. 1,3,4,5 ; Series 1, Vol. 39, Pt. 1,2,3; Series 1, Vol. 47, Pt. 2; Series 3, Vol. 5

"Zubley Family Papers." Morrow, GA: Georgia State Archives

The Author

Paulette Snoby is also the author of *April's Revolution: A Modern Perspective of American Medical Care of Civil War Soldiers and African Slaves.* For more information about Paulette, please visit: www.CWAtlantaNurse.com

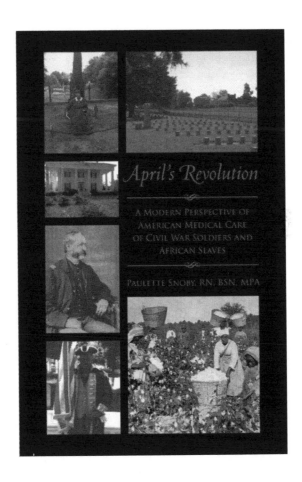

25502309R00098

Made in the USA
San Bernardino, CA
02 November 2015